THE IDIOM ADVENTURE

FLUENCY IN SPEAKING AND LISTENING

DANA WATKINS

The Idiom Adventure: Fluency in Speaking and Listening

Pearson Education, 10 Bank Street, White Plains, NY 10606

Vice president, director of publishing: Allen Asher
Editorial director: Louisa B. Hellegers
Acquisitions editor: Eleanor Barnes
Senior development manager: Penny Laporte
Development editor: Lise Minovitz
Vice president, director of design and production: Rhea Banker
Executive managing editor: Linda Moser
Senior manufacturing buyer: Dave Dickey
Production manager: Liza Pleva
Production editors: Martin Yu and Noël Vreeland Carter
Photo research: Frank M. Scalise
Cover design: Ann France
Text design: Curt Belshe, Quay Design
Text composition: Publication Services
Text art: Mona Daley
Photo credits: page 74, top, © Kevin Schafer/CORBIS; center, ©Roger Wood/CORBIS;
    bottom, © John Heseltine/CORBIS

Library of Congress Cataloging-in-Publication Data

Watkins, Dana
    The idiom adventure : fluency in speaking and listening / Dana Watkins.
      p. cm.
    ISBN 0-201-61992-X (alk. paper)
    1. English language—Textbooks for foreign speakers. 2. English language—Spoken
English—Problems, exercises, etc. 3. English language—Idioms—Problems, exercises, etc.
4. Listening—Problems, exercises, etc. I. Title.

PE1128, W367 2001
428.3'4–dc21

                                                    00-046455

CONTENTS

INTRODUCTION

TO THE TEACHER

Several years ago, I was teaching a course on idioms to speakers of other languages. I found the materials I was using dry and dull—and I could only imagine what my students thought of them!

In my view, idioms are anything but dry and dull. In fact, they are the most interesting and fun part of English, giving it character and spice. I felt that their sense of playfulness and inventiveness should be passed along to students.

At the time I was teaching the course on idioms, I noticed that common media materials—particularly magazine ads—were rich sources of idiomatic language. Easy to find, collect, and use, these ads were highly visual, short, focused, and "catchy." Moreover, they could be used to teach students reading, writing, speaking, listening, and critical thinking skills. They were also rich sources of information about American culture. I decided to expose my students to as many examples of idioms in authentic magazine ads as possible. The ads turned out to be a hit in my classroom. Learning idioms suddenly became fun!

That experience became the catalyst for writing my high-intermediate textbook, *The Idiom Advantage,* and later this intermediate textbook, *The Idiom Adventure.* In this book, I have tried to develop activities and exercises that engage and interest students, while helping them with the often confusing and difficult task of decoding idioms and learning how to use them appropriately. In addition, I have included some of the magazine ads that I have collected over the years. I believe these ads, which present authentic examples of the idioms, set this book apart.

Structure and Use of the Text

The Idiom Adventure has been written for intermediate students who have not yet mastered the mechanics of English. They are aware of idioms and may even use a few. However, it is unlikely that they are familiar enough with the language to identify and use idioms accurately. Therefore, I have provided a wide range of listening, speaking, reading, and writing activities to help the students learn and practice the idioms. As the teacher, you can decide which activities are most useful for your students. Choose those activities that focus on the language skills that you wish to target, and omit those that do not meet your students' needs.

Each of the twelve chapters is divided into three sections containing various listening, reading, speaking, and writing activities. The sequence and content of each section follows.

I. Learning the Idioms

WARMING UP

Communicative activities, such as games, problem-solving activities, and discussion questions, introduce the chapter topic. The students are encouraged to warm up, loosen up, and talk, talk, talk.

GETTING TO KNOW THE IDIOMS

This section consists of three interrelated exercises in which the students listen to, read, and define the idioms in the chapter.

A. Listening for Understanding: The idioms are introduced in a recorded passage from a radio or television program, a newspaper report, or a letter. The students listen for comprehension and discuss the topic without focusing on the idioms.

B. Identifying the Idioms: The recorded introductory passage is presented in script form. The students read the script and guess the general meaning of each idiom from its context.

C. Getting the Meaning: The idioms are presented in new contexts. The students match each idiom with its correct definition.

PRACTICING THE IDIOMS

This section consists of three exercises in which the students encounter the idioms in new contexts and practice using them in structured activities.

D. Choosing the Best Answer: The students listen to recorded statements or conversations that include the idioms or their synonyms. They choose the correct responses to true/false or multiple choice questions.

E. Retelling the Story: The students read statements that refer to the introductory passage, then paraphrase them using appropriate idioms.

F. Putting the Idioms into Practice: The students insert appropriate idioms into letters, interviews, or news reports. Some exercises have definite answers; other exercises allow more varied and creative responses.

II. Finding the Idioms in Ads

This section presents authentic magazine ads that feature idioms from the chapter. The students study the idioms in context and learn about aspects of American culture, such as humor, values, and politics.

INTERPRETING THE ADS

The students answer questions about each ad to determine its message.

THINKING ABOUT THE ADS

The students choose one ad from the chapter and analyze the relevance of its message to Americans and people in their own culture.

III. Using the Idioms

In this section, the students practice using the idioms creatively in less structured speaking and writing activities.

USING THE IDIOMS IN SPEECH

A. Name That Idiom: The students review the idioms from the chapter in a fast-paced game.

B. Round Robin Story: The students use the target idioms to create a group story.

C. Role Play: The students use idioms and characters from the introductory passage in a role play.

USING THE IDIOMS IN WRITING

D. Writing with Idioms: The students write e-mail messages, sales brochures, newspaper reports, or personal ads.

E. Advertising with Idioms: The students create and present an original ad campaign featuring an idiom from the chapter.

After each three chapters, a review section provides activities such as games, puzzles, and writing activities. The Glossary in the Appendix presents an alphabetical listing of the idioms with definitions, example sentences, and usage notes. The Audioscript and Answer Key provides audioscripts for the Choosing the Best Answer sections and answers to selected exercises.

TO THE STUDENT

Read the following expressions. Do you know what they mean?

a piece of cake	on a roll	go with the flow
nothing to sneeze at	eat one's words	for the birds

These expressions are *idioms*. An idiom is an expression that has a special meaning which is different than the *literal* meaning, or usual meaning. For example, the literal meanings of *piece* is "part" and of *cake* is "a kind of dessert," but the idiom *piece of cake* means "very easy."

You will learn the idioms above—and many more—as you study the lessons in this book. In addition, you will use them to talk and write about a variety of topics. Even more exciting, you will see the idioms in authentic magazine ads.

Try to notice idioms in American speech and writing. Even if you don't understand what they mean, recognizing that particular expressions are idioms is an important part of learning the language. Although idioms can be confusing, they also make English interesting.

Have fun with idioms! Don't be afraid of them, and don't hesitate to ask questions if you don't understand something. Soon, you will find that learning new idioms is *a piece of cake*.

Chapter 1

CAREER

Idioms

A BREEZE

COUCH POTATO

COUNT ON SOMEONE OR SOMETHING

DO SOMETHING FOR A LIVING

HAVE A GREEN THUMB

LEAVE WELL ENOUGH ALONE

MAKE SOMETHING FROM SCRATCH

RUN-OF-THE-MILL

No matter what you do for a living,
include music in your life.

I Learning the Idioms

WARMING UP

Complete the following activities in pairs or small groups. Compare answers and discuss with your classmates.

1. Play the game *Charades*.
   - Choose a job (e.g., doctor, pilot, teacher). Do not tell your classmates what it is.
   - Role-play the job in front of the group without talking.
   - Your classmates try to guess your job.
   - The first student to guess correctly chooses and role-plays the next job.

2. Play the game *What Am I?*
   - Choose a job. Do not tell your classmates what it is.
   - Your classmates try to guess your job by asking yes/no questions. (Examples: *Do you work in an office? Do you use a computer? Do you work with animals?*)
   - The first student to guess correctly chooses the next job.

3. Choose five jobs. Write at least three things needed for each job.
   (Example: *A fisherman needs a boat, a net, and a fishing rod.*)

4. Describe your ideal job. Discuss the following questions.
   - What is your ideal job? Why?
   - How important is salary to you?
   - Do you prefer to be the boss, have a boss, or be your own boss? Why?
   - Do you prefer to work alone or with others? Why?
   - Do you prefer to work in one place or travel for work? Why?

GETTING TO KNOW THE IDIOMS

A. Listening for Understanding

Listen to the TV game show What's My Job? *Think about the following questions. Then discuss your answers in pairs or small groups.*

1. What does Guest 1 do? Guest 2? Guest 3? Guest 4?

2. Which job do you think requires the most mental work?

3. Which job do you think requires the most physical work?

4. Who does Guest 4 have to depend on to do her job? Why?

5. Which job do you think is the best? Why?

B. Identifying the Idioms

The idioms listed below are used throughout the TV game show you just heard. Read the script of the TV game show on page 4. Underline the idioms. Number them on the list below in the order they occur. Try to guess the meaning of each idiom by looking at how it is used.

____ a breeze

____ couch potato

____ count on someone or something

____ do something for a living

____ have a green thumb

____ leave well enough alone

____ make something from scratch

____ run-of-the-mill

What's My Job?

HOST: What do you do for a living? Are you a banker, a soldier, a priest, a teacher? Maybe a taxi driver, a dentist, a cowboy, a farmer? Or perhaps you are a librarian, an athlete, or a musician? Today, on *What's My Job?*, you will meet four people with different occupations. Can you guess what they do for a living? Listen to them tell you about their jobs. Then try to guess what they do. Good luck!

GUEST 1: Hi, everybody! I have a wonderful job, because I make things that everyone loves! I wear a tall white hat and an apron, and I work in the kitchen. I make everything from scratch; I never use mixes from boxes or cans. Of course, my customers think everything I make is delicious. Can you guess what I am?

GUEST 2: Other people may enjoy their run-of-the-mill jobs, but not me! I have the most interesting job in the world! If you want to do what I do, you must be *very* creative. I am always thinking, trying to find new ways of doing things. While I'm walking or even talking to someone, I am still thinking and thinking. What new thing can I make to solve a problem? Or how can I make something better? I can never leave well enough alone—I always have to improve things in some way. People count on me to make their lives easier and more efficient. Can you guess what I am?

GUEST 3: I chose this occupation because I don't like working in an office. I don't like to answer phones or go to meetings or dress in a suit. I like to work outside, with nature. It's wonderful to put my hands in the dirt and to make the world more beautiful. To do what I do, some people say you must have a green thumb. They think it's hard to make plants and flowers grow. But I think it's a breeze! For me, it's easy. And it feels so good to work outdoors. Can you guess what I am?

GUEST 4: My job is very exciting. We travel to different places where we set up a big tent for our big shows. I work with clowns and animal trainers. You could never do my job if you were a couch potato—you must be very physically active. You can't be afraid of high places either. Sometimes I have to climb way up high and jump off. I must count on my partners to catch me. I hope they don't miss! Can you guess what I am?

C. Getting the Meaning

Look at the underlined phrase in each of the following statements. Pay attention to how the idiom is used, and try to guess its meaning. You may also refer to the script of What's My Job? *on page 4. Choose from the definitions below. Write the letter on the line.*

___b___   1. Amy is very active, but her husband is a <u>couch potato</u>.

_____   2. John is a pilot; flying is what he <u>does for a living</u>.

_____   3. I usually make cakes from mixes, but Becky always <u>makes hers from scratch</u>.

_____   4. I finished the math homework in ten minutes. It was <u>a breeze</u>!

_____   5. I can't prepare for the party alone. I'm <u>counting on you</u> to help.

_____   6. Have you seen Harriet's beautiful garden? She must <u>have a green thumb</u>.

_____   7. That restaurant serves <u>run-of-the-mill</u> food. It's nothing special.

_____   8. Your painting looks fine! Why don't you <u>leave well enough alone</u>?

a. to depend on someone or something

b. someone who spends a lot of time sitting and watching TV

c. to make something (especially food) with basic ingredients, rather than from a prepared mix

d. to do something as one's job

e. to have a special talent to make plants grow

f. to be satisfied with things as they are; to not try to improve things

g. very easy

h. ordinary; average

PRACTICING THE IDIOMS

D. Choosing the Best Answer

Listen to each statement. Read the sentences below. Choose the sentence that best matches the statement you heard. Circle a or b.

1. a. Brett watches a lot of television.
    (b.) Brett wants his children to be more active.
2. a. The Harrisons depended on the firefighters.
    b. The Harrisons knew how many firefighters would come.

3. a. For Evelyn, dancing is easy.
   b. Evelyn dances like the wind.

4. a. Kent lost money because he couldn't stop gambling.
   b. Kent had good luck gambling in Las Vegas.

5. a. Al wants to buy something that runs.
   b. Al wants to buy something special.

6. a. Ellen's roses were green.
   b. Ellen grew beautiful roses.

7. a. Almost everything Stewart cooks comes from a can.
   b. Stewart did not use a mix when he made lasagna.

8. a. Tony earned money by playing football, and then he opened a restaurant.
   b. Tony always ate at a restaurant after playing football.

E. Retelling the Story

Read the script of What's My Job? *on page 4 again. The sentences below refer to statements in that script. Restate the sentences, using the appropriate idioms. Try to write them* <u>without</u> *looking at the script again.*

1. What kind of job do you have?

   What do you do for a living?
   _____

2. Guest 1 makes all his food from basic ingredients.

   _____

3. Some people may like ordinary jobs, but not Guest 2.

   _____

4. Guest 2 is not satisfied if she doesn't try to improve things.

   _____

5. Everyone depends on Guest 2 to make life easier.

   _____

6. To do Guest 3's job, you must have a special ability to make plants grow.

   _____

7. Guest 3 thinks his job is easy.

   _____

8. You can't do Guest 4's job if you spend a lot of time just sitting and watching television.

   _____

9. Guest 4 depends on her partners to catch her when she jumps from high places.

   _____

F. Putting the Idioms into Practice

Imagine that you have an interview for a job at a bakery. Read the manager's questions. Answer the questions, using the idioms indicated. Change the form of the idioms as needed to fit your answers.

MANAGER: Can you tell me about your last job?

YOU: _____ I had a run-of-the-mill job. I worked in a factory. _____
   1. run-of-the-mill

MANAGER: We don't want to hire lazy people. How would you describe yourself?

YOU: _____
   2. couch potato

MANAGER: We're always trying to make new pastries, so you must have some experience working in a kitchen. Do you enjoy cooking?

YOU: _____
   3. make something from scratch

MANAGER: We also have some popular recipes that we don't want to change. Will that be a problem?

YOU: _____
   4. leave well enough alone

MANAGER: Can we depend on you to arrive on time and work hard?

YOU: _____
   5. count on someone

MANAGER: Do you think you can do this job?

YOU: _____
   6. a breeze

MANAGER: What kind of career would you like to have?

YOU: _____
   7. do something for a living

MANAGER: Do you have any hobbies or special interests outside of work?

YOU: _____
   8. have a green thumb

II Finding the Idioms in Ads

INTERPRETING THE ADS

Look at the following ads. Determine what is being advertised. Find the featured idiom in each ad and review its meaning. Then answer the questions.

1983 "From the road to the roof it's laced with intriguing tidbits and thoughtful touches." *Car and Driver*

1984 "The new front-drive Camry 4-door sedan offers comfort, quality, and interior space in generous portions." *Motor Trend*

1985 "Most trouble-free new car in America."* *J.D. Power and Associates*

1986 "Best Buy" *Consumers Digest*

1987 "If the world's auto manufacturers were only allowed to build one car to satisfy the needs of all car buyers everywhere, the Camry would be the logical choice." *Motor Trend*

1988 "The Camry is everything a family car should be." *Car and Driver*

1989 "Family Car of the Year." *Family Circle Magazine*

1990 "Most trouble-free compact car in America three years in a row."* *J.D. Power and Associates*

1991 "Ranked in J.D. Power and Associates Top Ten models in Initial Quality."* *J.D. Power and Associates*

1992. WE JUST COULDN'T LEAVE WELL ENOUGH ALONE.

THE ALL-NEW 1992 CAMRY

"I love what you do for me."

J.D. Power and Associates 1985, 1988, 1989, 1990 and 1991 Initial Quality Surveys. Based on owner reported problems during the first 90 days of ownership. Call 1-800-GO-TOYOTA for a brochure and location of your nearest dealer. Get More From Life....Buckle Up! © 1991 Toyota Motor Sales, U.S.A., Inc.

TOYOTA

Reprinted with the permission of Toyota Motor Sales, U.S.A. Inc.

1. Quotes from different magazines are at the top of the ad. What do they say?

2. Calling the car *all-new* suggests that it has been changed. How does this relate to the slogan[1] *We just couldn't leave well enough alone*?

3. What is the message of this ad?

---

[1]a short, memorable phrase used in an ad to get people's attention

1. What is a *couch potato*?

2. *Small fry* means "children." Explain the slogan *Prevent couch potatoes while they're still small fries.*

3. What is the usual meaning of *fries*? What are french fries made from?

PREVENT COUCH POTATOES WHILE THEY'RE STILL SMALL FRIES.

Now is the time to teach your kids good habits. Like eating low-fat, low-cholesterol foods. And getting plenty of exercise. You might save wear and tear on their hearts. And on your chair. You can help prevent heart disease and stroke. We can tell you how. Call 1-800-AHA-USA1.

American Heart Association ❤

This space provided as a public service. ©1993, American Heart Association.

©Reproduced with permission, *Prevent Couch Potatoes While They're Still Small Fries,* 1993. Copyright American Heart Association.

NOW YOU CAN MAKE YOUR COOKTOP FROM SCRATCH, TOO.

INTRODUCING THE NEW KITCHENAID® CREATE-A-COOKTOP SYSTEM. THE INGREDIENTS: ELECTRIC GRILL, TWO-BURNER SEALED GAS UNIT, ELECTRIC UNIT WITH TWO CAST-IRON ELEMENTS, GLASS CERAMIC RADIANT/HALOGEN UNIT, DOWNDRAFT VENT. IN YOUR CHOICE OF BLACK, WHITE OR ALMOND.

MIX OR MATCH THE UNITS TO CREATE A COOKTOP THAT MATCHES THE WAY YOU COOK. CREATE ONE BIG COOKTOP. OR CREATE TWO SEPARATE COOKING STATIONS. CREATE A SEPARATE WARMING STATION. OR CREATE A SEPARATE GRILLING AREA. USE THE SLEEK DOWNDRAFT VENT OR AN OVERHEAD EXHAUST SYSTEM.

NO MATTER HOW YOU DESIGN IT, YOU'LL GET THE SAME PREMIUM QUALITY THAT HAS MADE KITCHENAID DISHWASHERS LEGENDARY.

TO START CREATING YOUR COOKTOP, JUST CALL THE KITCHENAID CONSUMER ASSISTANCE CENTER, 1-800-422-1230, FOR INFORMATION AND THE NAME OF THE DEALER NEAREST YOU.

KitchenAid®
FOR THE WAY IT'S MADE.®

®REGISTERED TRADEMARK/™TRADEMARK OF KITCHENAID   ©1992 KITCHENAID

Reprinted with the permission of KitchenAid.

1. Describe the picture. What is being advertised?

2. How is this cooktop different from other cooktops?

3. Usually food is *made from scratch*. In what way can a cooktop be *made from scratch*?

Bound

to make

healthy living a breeze.

Keep your issues of COOKING LIGHT easily accessible with the COOKING LIGHT Binder or Issue Case. Each is manufactured from heavy reinforced board to keep your magazines protected, and we've stamped both with the COOKING LIGHT logo in metallic gold. Whether you choose cases or binders, you'll have a storage system that's durable and well-organized—keeping a full year (10 issues) right at your fingertips. To order your COOKING LIGHT Binders or Issue Cases at $9.95 each, just call the toll-free number listed below. Or send us your name and address, specifying your choice of binders or issue cases, along with a check or money order payable to COOKING LIGHT Collection. It's that simple! Please add $3.95 per order for postage/handling. Send your order today to: COOKING LIGHT Collection, P.O. Box 830817, Birmingham, AL 35283-0817.

CALL 1-800-522-9476 TO ORDER

Reprinted with the permission of Southern Progress Corporation.

1. *Bound to* means "certain to." How is the magazine, *Cooking Light,* certain to make healthy living *a breeze*?

2. Describe the picture. How does it relate to the idiom in this ad?

No matter what you do for a living, include music in your life.

Boeing controls all rights.

1. Describe the picture.

2. Boeing is a company that makes airplanes. However, it is not advertising airplanes in this ad. What do you think it's promoting?

1. What is Jason Harrington's job? Does he need *a green thumb* to do his job?

2. The ad explains Jason Harrington's accident. He lost his thumb and two fingers. Doctors at USC University Hospital replaced his thumb with his big toe so that he could regain use of his hand. Explain the slogan *Jason Harrington's green thumb is courtesy of his big toe.*

Reprinted with the permission of USC University Hospital.

THINKING ABOUT THE ADS

Review the ads in this chapter. Choose the one that you like best. Complete the following statements based on that ad.

1. The ad that I like the best is . . . because . . . .

2. I think Americans would like this ad because . . . .

3. It is important to many Americans to . . . .

4. Other examples in American life that show how Americans feel about this value are . . . .

5. People from my country would/would not like this ad because . . . .

III Using the Idioms

USING THE IDIOMS IN SPEECH

A. Name That Idiom!

Play the following game in pairs. Try to be the first pair in your class to finish.

1. With a partner, copy the idioms from the list on page 1 onto separate index cards.

2. Divide the cards into two piles. Give one pile to your partner. Do not look at each other's cards.

3. Choose one card from your pile. Give a definition of the idiom or a sentence that illustrates its meaning <u>without</u> using the idiom.

4. After identifying the idiom correctly, your partner chooses a card from his or her pile and gives a definition or sentence.

5. Continue back and forth until you and your partner have correctly guessed all the idioms.

B. Round-Robin Story

Complete the following story in small groups.

1. One student adds to the story that begins below, using one of the idioms from this chapter.

2. The next student continues the story, using another idiom from this chapter.

3. Continue until all the idioms have been used and the story has ended.

   All her life, it seemed, Josie had done only what other people wanted her to do. When she was a child, she did what her parents wanted. When she was in school, she did what her teachers wanted. When she worked, she did what her boss wanted. Now Josie was ready to change that. Josie had a dream of doing something different for a living. She wanted to . . . .

C. Role Play

Perform a role play in pairs.

1. Imagine that you are one of the characters below. You may refer to the script of *What's My Job?* on page 4 for background information.

2. Write a script for a role play. Use as many of the idioms from this chapter as you can.

3. Practice the role play.

4. Perform the role play for your classmates.

COOK: You think your job is best. Tell the gardener why.

GARDENER: You think your job is best. Tell the cook why.

USING THE IDIOMS IN WRITING

D. Writing with Idioms

Have you ever had an interesting job? Can you imagine a job you would like, even if it seems impossible (e.g., a queen, a rock-and-roll star, or a professional soccer player)?

1. Write a description of the job. Use at least four idioms from this chapter, but do not write the name of the job.

2. Exchange papers with a partner. Try to guess what job he or she described.

3. Make suggestions about how to improve each other's descriptions.

E. Advertising with Idioms

Create an ad for a product or service.

1. Choose a product or service that you would like to advertise.

2. Determine your audience—the people most likely to buy your product or service.

3. Write a slogan for your ad, using one or more of the idioms from this chapter.

4. Decide what picture(s) you will use in your ad.

5. Write the rest of your ad.

6. Present your ad to the class. Do your classmates understand your use of the idiom? Would they buy your product or service?

Chapter 2

DEBATE

Idioms

- A PIECE OF CAKE
- KICK THE HABIT
- LIGHTEN UP
- OUT OF STEP
- SEE RED
- TO EACH HIS OWN
- **UP IN ARMS**
- WORK ONESELF INTO A LATHER

You don't have to get up in arms to visit a GM Goodwrench dealer.

Some women come in for service dressed for battle. Literally. They're tired of being talked down to, ignored and bullied about their cars. But there's a simple solution. Your GM Goodwrench® dealership. With GM training, tools, equipment and genuine GM parts, it just makes sense that they'd know how to take care of your car or light truck. And because GM Goodwrench dealers want to earn your loyalty, they also know how to take care of you. With honesty and courtesy. So don't let your car's need for routine maintenance turn into an ongoing battle. Pay a friendly visit to your GM Goodwrench dealer. Just call 1-800-GM USE US for one near you. And come as you are.

Goodwrench
We want your business.

CHEVROLET • PONTIAC • OLDSMOBILE • BUICK • CADILLAC • GMC TRUCK

©1994 GM Corp. All rights reserved.

I Learning the Idioms

WARMING UP

Complete the following activities in pairs or small groups. Compare answers and discuss with your classmates.

1. Discuss the following questions.
   - Do you smoke?
   - Does anyone in your family smoke?
   - Does it bother you if the people around you smoke?
   - What is your attitude toward smokers?

2. Which of the following is the worst for your health? Rank them from 1 (bad) to 6 (worst). Compare your answers.

   ____ smoking cigarettes   ____ eating too much junk food

   ____ taking illegal drugs   ____ getting too little sleep

   ____ drinking too much alcohol   ____ getting too little exercise

3. Discuss the following statements. Do you agree or disagree? Why?
   - Smoking in public places should not be allowed.
   - Tobacco and alcohol companies should pay to treat the illnesses that result from using their products.
   - Smoking cigarettes and drinking alcohol should be illegal for pregnant women.
   - Employers should have the right to perform random drug tests on employees.
   - There should be a special tax on junk food to discourage people from eating it.

GETTING TO KNOW THE IDIOMS

A. Listening for Understanding

Listen to the radio talk show Point . . . Counterpoint. *Think about the following questions. Then discuss your answers in pairs or small groups.*

1. What is *Point . . . Counterpoint?*

2. Which of the two guests on the show smokes? How do you know?

3. What does Mr. Merrick think of the controversy over smoking?

4. What does Ms. Schwartz think?

5. Do you think that someday smoking will become illegal? Why?

B. Identifying the Idioms

The idioms listed below are used throughout the radio talk show you just heard. Read the script of the radio talk show on page 17. Underline the idioms. Number them on the list below in the order they occur. Try to guess the meaning of each idiom by looking at how it is used.

_____ a piece of cake   _____ see red

_____ kick the habit   _____ to each his own

_____ lighten up   _____ up in arms

_____ out of step   _____ work oneself into a lather

Point . . . Counterpoint

HOST: Welcome, ladies and gentlemen, to *Point . . . Counterpoint*, where we are not afraid to discuss the hottest and most controversial topics of our time. On today's show we will introduce to you Mr. Joseph Merrick and Ms. Carolyn Schwartz, who hold opposing viewpoints on the issue of smoking in public. Now, everyone knows that it's not a healthy habit, and some people believe that smoking should not be allowed anywhere in public. What do you think? Should smokers be allowed to smoke in public places? First, let's hear from Mr. Merrick. What do you have to say, sir?

MERRICK: I say, "Lighten up!" Everyone is much too serious about this whole issue!

SCHWARTZ: Excuse me, Mr. Merrick, but did you say "lighten up" or "light up"? This **is** a serious issue. It's not just your health I'm worried about, it's mine! When a smoker lights up around me, I see red! It makes me angry to have to breathe someone else's smoke!

MERRICK: Don't work yourself into a lather! That's the problem with you nonsmokers. You get so upset over a little puff of smoke. If I want to smoke, I should have that right. To each his own!

SCHWARTZ: Maybe you should be able to smoke if you want to, but only in your own home. If I am up in arms over people smoking in public, it's because I don't want to be forced to breathe their cigarette smoke.

MERRICK: Relax! A little bit of smoke isn't going to hurt you!

SCHWARTZ: What?! Yes, it is! You're completely out of step if you believe it can't hurt you. Why don't you just kick the habit? You'd be in much better health if you quit.

MERRICK: You think quitting smoking is a piece of cake? Well, it's not! It's hard. I've tried many times. People like you don't understand smokers at all.

HOST: That's all we have time for. Thank you, Mr. Merrick and Ms. Schwartz, for sharing your views with us. Now it's time for you, the public, to tell us what you think. Should people be able to smoke in public? Should there be laws against it? Do you think cigarette smoking should be a criminal offense? Let us know here on *Point . . . Counterpoint*.

C. Getting the Meaning

Look at the underlined phrase in each of the following statements. Pay attention to how the idiom is used, and try to guess its meaning. You may also refer to the script of Point . . . Counterpoint *on page 17. Choose from the definitions below. Write the letter on the line.*

__b__   1. When my son told me that he'd lost his new jacket, I <u>saw red</u>.

_____   2. If Randy wants to get a tattoo and pierce his nose, let him. <u>To each his own</u>.

_____   3. The English test was <u>a piece of cake</u>! I got all the answers right.

_____   4. The factory workers are <u>up in arms</u> because their pay was cut.

_____   5. I can't understand why you're so upset. <u>Lighten up</u>!

_____   6. I know I shouldn't bite my fingernails, but I just can't <u>kick the habit</u>.

_____   7. Bonnie <u>worked herself into a lather</u> when her children returned home late.

_____   8. Annie is often <u>out of step</u> with her friends. They like rock music, but she prefers jazz.

a. to quit an addictive behavior pattern

b. to become very angry

c. different from usual beliefs or behavior

d. very easy

e. to become agitated or angry about something others consider unimportant

f. to relax; to not get upset

g. allow everyone his or her own preferences

h. very angry and ready to fight

PRACTICING THE IDIOMS

D. Choosing the Best Answer

Listen to the questions and statements. Read the sentences below. Choose the best response to the question or statement you heard. Circle a or b.

1. a. It was a piece of cake.
     (b.) She saw red.

2. a. Definitely. Women will be up in arms soon if there isn't someone to represent them.
     b. Yes. Women are out of step with politics.

3. a. Parties make me see red.
     b. Lighten up! It's not that important.

4. a. To each his own.
   b. They should kick the habit.

5. a. For her, it's a piece of cake.
   b. She is up in arms over her English class.

6. a. Yes, she worked herself into a lather.
   b. Yes, she said, "To each his own."

7. a. He should lighten up.
   b. He is out of step with the other workers.

8. a. Henry kicked the habit.
   b. Henry was up in arms.

E. Retelling the Story

Read the script of Point . . . Counterpoint *on page 17 again. The sentences below refer to statements in that script. Restate the sentences, using the appropriate idioms. Try to write them* <u>without</u> *looking at the script again.*

1. Mr. Merrick thought that everyone was too serious about smoking and that they should relax.

   _____Mr. Merrick said that everyone should lighten up_____

2. Every time someone near Ms. Schwartz lights up a cigarette, she gets angry.

   _____

3. Mr. Merrick told her not to get so angry.

   _____

4. He believes that everyone should be allowed his or her own preferences.

   _____

5. Ms. Schwartz said she is ready to fight when people smoke in public because she doesn't like to breathe their smoke.

   _____

6. She told him that if he believes cigarette smoke is harmless, his beliefs are very different from those of other people.

   _____

7. She asked Mr. Merrick why he doesn't just quit smoking.

   _____

8. Mr. Merrick said that quitting is not easy.

   _____

F. Putting the Idioms into Practice

Read the statements below. Complete each statement with the appropriate idiom from the list. Circle AGREE if you agree with the statement or DISAGREE if you disagree.

a piece of cake	**see red**
kick the habit	**to each his own**
lighten up	**up in arms**
out of step	**work themselves into a lather**

1. When I see an adult spanking a child, I _____ see red _____. It makes me angry because it teaches children that it's OK to hit others.

   AGREE   DISAGREE

2. Parents have different ways of disciplining their children, and no one else should interfere. If some parents think that spanking is best, that's fine. _____.

   AGREE   DISAGREE

3. Marijuana is not a harmful drug. Everyone should _____ and not be so serious about it. It should be legalized.

   AGREE   DISAGREE

4. Anyone who thinks that marijuana should be legal is _____ with the rest of society. It's a harmful drug.

   AGREE   DISAGREE

5. Smoking is a bad habit that hurts everyone. People who smoke should
_____. Everyone would be healthier without cigarettes
around.

AGREE   DISAGREE

6. The stress that nonsmokers experience when they get angry at smokers is probably
worse for their health than smoking. When they _____,
they're only hurting themselves.

AGREE   DISAGREE

7. There's no excuse for illiteracy. Every school-age child in the world should know
how to read. Reading is not hard; it's _____.

AGREE   DISAGREE

8. People shouldn't get _____ over illiteracy. There are
places where reading isn't necessary to survive. It's more important to provide food
and medicine to everyone on earth.

AGREE   DISAGREE

II Finding the Idioms in Ads

INTERPRETING THE ADS

Look at the following ads. Determine what is being advertised. Find the featured idiom in each ad and review its meaning. Then answer the questions.

Proctor & Gamble

1. What is *static*?

2. What is happening in the picture?

3. How could static put you *out of step*?

1. Describe the picture.

2. What does Resolve do?

3. What is the message of this ad?

Reprinted with permission of Reckitt & Colman, Inc.

Reprinted with the permission of Sanyo Presentation Technologies.

1. Describe the picture. What is the goose carrying? Is it light or heavy?

2. A feature of this product is its light weight. How does this relate to the phrase *lighten up*?

3. Is the phrase *lighten up* used literally,[1] idiomatically,[2] or both? Explain.

---

[1] related to the usual meaning of a word or phrase
[2] related to the special meaning of an idiom

You don't have to get up in arms
to visit a GM Goodwrench dealer.

Some women come in for service dressed for battle. Literally. They're tired of being
talked down to, ignored and bullied about their cars. But there's a simple solution. Your
GM Goodwrench® dealership. With GM training, tools, equipment and genuine GM parts,
it just makes sense that they'd know how to take care of your car or light truck.
And because GM Goodwrench dealers want to earn your loyalty, they also know how to
take care of you. With honesty and courtesy. So don't let your car's need for routine
maintenance turn into an ongoing battle. Pay a friendly visit to your GM Goodwrench dealer.
Just call **1-800-GM USE US** for one near you. And come as you are.

Goodwrench
We want your business.

CHEVROLET • PONTIAC • OLDSMOBILE • BUICK • CADILLAC • GMC TRUCK

1. Describe the picture. What is the woman wearing?

2. The audience for this ad consists of women who don't like the way car mechanics have behaved toward them. What is the message of this ad?

3. The literal meaning of *up in arms* is "to be ready to fight with weapons." In this ad, is the phrase used literally, idiomatically, or both? Explain.

1. What does *lather* mean?

2. What is being advertised? How is it related to lather?

3. Is the phrase *work yourself into a lather* used literally, idiomatically, or both? Explain.

1. What items are pictured in this ad? What color do you think they are in the original ad?

2. What is being advertised? Who do you think the audience is?

3. According to the ad, children will stain their clothes with anything red. How would that make someone *see red*?

4. Explain the two meanings of *How to avoid seeing red*.

Proctor & Gamble

THINKING ABOUT THE ADS

Review the ads in this chapter. Choose the one that you like best. Complete the following statements based on that ad.

1. The ad that I like the best is . . . because . . . .

2. I think Americans would like this ad because . . . .

3. It is important to many Americans to . . . .

4. Other examples in American life that show how Americans feel about this value are . . . .

5. People from my country would/would not like this ad because . . . .

III Using the Idioms

USING THE IDIOMS IN SPEECH

A. Name That Idiom!

Play the following game in pairs. Try to be the first pair in your class to finish.

1. With a partner, copy the idioms from the list on page 14 onto separate index cards.

2. Divide the cards into two piles. Give one pile to your partner. Do not look at each other's cards.

3. Choose one card from your pile. Give a definition of the idiom or a sentence that illustrates its meaning <u>without</u> using the idiom.

4. After identifying the idiom correctly, your partner chooses a card from his or her pile and gives a definition or sentence.

5. Continue back and forth until you and your partner have correctly guessed all the idioms.

B. Round-Robin Story

Complete the following story in small groups.

1. One student adds to the story that begins below, using one of the idioms from this chapter.

2. The next student continues the story, using another idiom from this chapter.

3. Continue until all the idioms have been used and the story has ended.

   Jim Evans, the supervisor at the Pacific Computer Company, was very concerned. His best worker, Bob Kimmel, usually did an excellent job. But lately, Bob had been coming to work with alcohol on his breath. Jim knew that Bob drank too much. Bob said he was trying to kick the habit, but nothing had changed. Finally, Mr. Evans decided . . . .

C. Role Play

Perform a role play in pairs.

1. Imagine that you are one of the characters at the top of page 27. It is one year after you appeared on the talk show *Point . . . Counterpoint*. You may refer to the script of *Point . . . Counterpoint* on page 17 for background information.

2. Write a script for a role play. Use as many of the idioms from this chapter as you can.

3. Practice the role play.

4. Perform the role play for your classmates.

MR. MERRICK: You have finally quit smoking. Explain how you did it. Now you are worried because your teenage daughter has started smoking. Discuss this problem.

MS. SCHWARTZ: Ask Mr. Merrick how he quit smoking. Give him advice about his daughter.

USING THE IDIOMS IN WRITING

D. Writing with Idioms

While most children in cities have used computers for many years, the majority of students at Mountain City School have no computer experience. The students' parents think they need to learn computer skills so they will have the same advantages as students in other schools. However, the teachers insist that computers are not necessary for a good education.

1. Imagine that you are the parent of a student at Mountain City School. Write a letter to your child's teacher. Explain why you think students need to learn computer skills. Include the following information.

   • You are very angry that the students are not being taught computer skills.

   • All the parents will be angry and ready to fight if the school does not provide computer classes.

   • The teachers' beliefs are very different from those of most people.

   Use at least two idioms from this chapter in your letter.

2. Imagine that you are the teacher who has just read the above letter. Respond to the letter. Include the following information.

   • There is no reason to get so angry about this issue.

   • You believe that other skills are more important, but everyone has his or her own preferences.

   • You don't think it will be hard for students to learn computer skills later because they're so easy.

   • The children are still very young and should have fun.

   Use at least two idioms from this chapter in your letter.

E. Advertising with Idioms

Create an ad for a product or service.

1. Choose a product or service that you would like to advertise.

2. Determine your audience—the people most likely to buy your product or service.

3. Write a slogan for your ad, using one or more of the idioms from this chapter.

4. Decide on what picture(s) you will use in your ad.

5. Write the rest of your ad.

6. Present your ad to the class. Do your classmates understand your use of the idiom? Would they buy your product or service?

Chapter 3

LOVE

Idioms

COME OUT OF ONE'S SHELL

GO OUT OF ONE'S WAY

HANG OUT

KNOCK ONE'S SOCKS OFF

NOT ONE'S CUP OF TEA

PICK UP THE TAB

TURN DOWN

WHAT MAKES SOMEONE TICK

OBVIOUSLY, WE KNOW WHAT MAKES PEOPLE TICK.

WE DIDN'T ACTUALLY INTEND TO MAKE SO MANY DIFFERENT WATCHES. IT JUST TOOK US A WHILE TO FIGURE OUT THE ONE YOU HAD IN MIND. 392 INDIVIDUAL WATCHES FROM $50 TO $300. **PULSAR**

© Disney

Pulsar is a registered trademark of SEIKO CORPORATION. Disney characters © Disney Enterprises, Inc. Used by permission from Disney Enterprises, Inc.

I Learning the Idioms

WARMING UP

Complete the following activities in pairs or small groups. Compare answers and discuss with your classmates.

1. Clark is a single 35-year-old banker. He would like to find someone to marry soon. He enjoys meeting different people, playing games (especially chess), listening to music, and reading books on finance. His hobbies include collecting wine and traveling. Recently, at a party, he met the three women described below. He can ask only one of them out on a date. Which one should he call? Why? Discuss your answers.

   • **Jill Mitchell, twenty-six years old, student of French at UCLA:** Jill loves to travel and go shopping. She lived in Paris for two years and in Tahiti for six months. Her hobbies include going to the ballet, collecting wine, and writing poetry.

   • **Marilyn McKay, thirty-seven years old, bank executive and financial expert:** Marilyn is divorced and has a sixteen-year-old son. She loves working at her job, meeting people, having parties, and watching old movies. Her hobbies include cooking, singing, and playing chess.

   • **Patricia Lever, thirty years old, photographer:** Patricia has traveled to almost every state in the United States. She loves to take pictures of people and places throughout the country. Her hobbies are collecting games and music from around the world.

2. If single, describe your ideal wife or husband. If married, explain why you married your husband or wife.

3. Have you ever had a memorable or unusual date? If so, describe it.

GETTING TO KNOW THE IDIOMS

A. Listening for Understanding

Listen to the TV game show The Matchmaking Game. *Think about the following questions. Then discuss your answers in pairs or small groups.*

1. What does Vivian like to do in her free time? What kind of man does she like?

2. What does Bachelor 1 think they should do together?

3. Does Vivian like to go to hockey games?

4. What idea does Bachelor 2 have for their date? Who does he think should pay for this date?

5. Describe Bachelor 3. Do you know anyone similar to him?

6. Who does Vivian choose to go out with? Why? Do you agree with her choice?

B. Identifying the Idioms

The idioms listed below are used throughout the TV game show you just heard. Read the script of the TV game show on page 32. Underline the idioms. Number them on the list in the order they occur. Try to guess the meaning of each idiom by looking at how it is used.

____ come out of one's shell   ____ not one's cup of tea

____ go out of one's way   ____ pick up the tab

____ hang out   ____ turn down

____ knock one's socks off   ____ what makes someone tick

The Matchmaking Game

HOST: Welcome to *The Matchmaking Game*! On today's show you will meet Vivian Porter, a twenty-three-year-old nurse from Chicago. Vivian likes to hang out in art museums when she's not working and says she loves men who go out of their way to make every date special. Today, Vivian will meet three bachelors who are hidden behind a screen. She can't see them, but she can ask them questions. At the end of our show, Vivian will select one of the three bachelors to go out with on a date. Vivian, what would you like to ask the bachelors?

VIVIAN: Bachelor Number 1, I am a little bit shy around people I don't know. What would you do to help me come out of my shell?

BACHELOR 1:   Oh, that's easy. I would take you to a hockey game! You'll be yelling as loud as the rest of us in no time!

VIVIAN: Well, hockey isn't really my cup of tea. Bachelor Number 2, what would you do?

BACHELOR 2:   I'm a lot more romantic than Bachelor Number 1. We could start with an art exhibit, then have a quiet dinner followed by an evening at the opera.

VIVIAN: That sounds lovely but quite expensive. Who would pick up the tab for this date?

BACHELOR 2:   I would, of course! I want to make this date impossible to turn down. I'd really love to go out with you.

VIVIAN: Thank you, Bachelor Number 2. Bachelor Number 3, if you were in a room full of people I didn't know, how would I recognize you?

BACHELOR 3:   Oh, baby, you'd know me for sure! One look at me will knock your socks off. Everyone notices me when I walk into a room. I'm definitely the best-looking guy here.

VIVIAN: Is that right? Well, we'll soon see about that.

HOST: OK, Vivian, now it's time to choose. Will it be Bachelor Number 1, Bachelor Number 2, or Bachelor Number 3?

VIVIAN: Bachelor Number 2. I'd like to spend some time getting to know him. He seems very thoughtful, and we like to do the same things. I want to know what makes him tick.

C. Getting the Meaning

Look at the underlined phrase in each of the following statements. Pay attention to how the idiom is used, and try to guess its meaning. You may also refer to the script of The Matchmaking Game *on page 32. Choose from the definitions below. Write the letter on the line.*

<u>c</u>   1. During the summer, my friends and I always <u>hang out</u> at the beach.

_____   2. Jan seemed quiet, but when she began to talk about her travels, she really <u>came out of her shell</u>.

_____   3. When Jerry and Diane go out for dinner, Diane always <u>picks up the tab</u>.

_____   4. Mark is such a strange man. I can't understand <u>what makes him tick</u>.

_____   5. I'd rather go to a rock concert than the symphony. Classical music is <u>not my cup of tea</u>.

_____   6. On our trip to Spain, the people were very willing to <u>go out of their way</u> to help us.

_____   7. The violinist at the concert <u>knocked my socks off</u>. She was great!

_____   8. I applied for a job with that company, but the boss <u>turned me down</u>.

a. to greatly impress one

b. to pay for something

c. to spend time

d. to make a special effort

e. what makes someone behave in a particular way

f. to refuse or reject something

g. not something one enjoys very much

h. to become less shy and more sociable

PRACTICING THE IDIOMS

D. Choosing the Best Answer

First listen to the telephone conversation between Michael and Judy. Then listen to each part of the conversation and to the questions that follow. Read the sentences below. Choose the sentence that best answers each question you heard. Circle a or b.

Part A

1. a. He picked up the tab for her packages.
    b. He went out of his way to help her.

2. a. He hangs out at home a lot.
    b. He never turns down a party invitation.

3. a. Going to parties isn't her cup of tea.
    b. A good party will knock her socks off.

Part B

4. a. He wants to know what makes Judy tick.
    b. He wants to know where to hang out.

5. a. He picks up the tab.
    b. He comes out of his shell.

6. a. She turns down the invitation.
    b. She goes out of her way to go to the party.

Part C

7. a. He thinks she will come out of her shell.
    b. He thinks she will knock Judy's socks off.

8. a. He will turn them down.
    b. He will pick up the tab.

E. Retelling the Story

Read the script of The Matchmaking Game *on page 32 again. The sentences below refer to statements in that script. Restate the sentences, using the appropriate idioms. Try to write them __without__ looking at the script again.*

1. Vivian enjoys spending her free time in art museums.

    Vivian likes to hang out in art museums.

2. Vivian likes men who really try to make every date special.

3. Vivian asked Bachelor Number 1 how he would help her be less shy.

_____

4. Vivian said that hockey was not an activity that she really enjoyed.

_____

5. Vivian wondered who would pay for the activities Bachelor Number 2 suggested.

_____

6. Bachelor Number 2 wanted to make his date impossible to refuse.

_____

7. Bachelor Number 3 said that his handsome appearance really impresses people.

_____

8. Vivian wants to get to know Bachelor Number 2 better.

_____

F. Putting the Idioms into Practice

Sometimes people try to find dates by placing personal ads in newspapers. Read the personal ads below. Replace the underlined word or phrase in each ad with an appropriate idiom from the list.

come out of your shell	**turn me down**
go out of her way	**what makes you tick**
knock your socks off	**hang out**
pick up the tab	**are not my cup of tea**

1. A very special woman is willing to <u>make every effort</u> to please her man. If you're a handsome gentleman, please respond quickly. I'm waiting for you!

    go out of her way
_____

2. Are you a fun-loving older woman? Young women <u>are not for me</u>, but if you are over fifty and love to dance, walk on the beach, and listen to opera, I'm your man!

_____

3. Are you shy? Give me a try! I will help you become more wild and adventurous. Call me if you want to <u>talk and laugh more</u>.

_____

4. Wealthy woman looking for handsome young man. I'm willing to <u>pay</u> for a wonderful time together. Let's go on a cruise or fly around the world!

_____

5. Do you love soft music, sunsets, and romantic movies? I'm a sensitive, kind woman looking for a man with a good heart. If that's you, then I want to <u>spend time</u> with you.

_____

6. Call me if you want to have a fabulous time with an amazing man. I will <u>greatly impress you</u> with my sense of humor and spirit of adventure.

_____

7. You won't <u>say no to me</u> when you discover what an interesting woman I am. I love good books, cats, good food, and my friends. Call me if you'd like to be one of them.

_____

8. If you are an unusual man, I want to know <u>all about you</u>. I am creative and artistic, and I want someone to share my thoughts with. Wouldn't you like to know me better?

_____

II Finding the Idioms in Ads

INTERPRETING THE ADS

Look at the following ads. Determine what is being advertised. Find the featured idiom in each ad and review its meaning. Then answer the questions.

1. Describe the top picture. Describe the bottom picture. Which do you think looks more interesting? Why?

2. Does the idiom apply to the bottom picture literally, idiomatically, or both?

3. Who is the audience for this ad?

Pulsar is a registered trademark of SEIKO CORPORATION.
Disney characters © Disney Enterprises, Inc. Used by
permission from Disney Enterprises, Inc.

1. What sound does a watch
   or clock make?

2. Why are there many
   different kinds of watches
   in the picture?

3. How does the picture
   relate to the idiom?

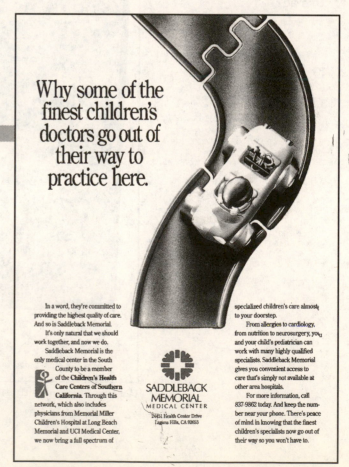

1. How do doctors *go out of
   their way* to help people?

2. This ad is for a hospital.
   Why do you think doctors
   go out of their way to work
   here?

Reprinted with the permission of Saddleback Memorial Medical Center.

1. This ad is for a cereal bar called *Nutri-Grain Twists*. Describe the bar.

2. The idiom in this ad is twisted, too. What is the correct idiom? How has it been changed in this ad?

3. The idiom *to go* refers to food bought in a restaurant and taken away to be eaten. Explain the phrase *Good food to go.*

1. What is *cable television*? How is it different from regular television? What kinds of cable channels are there?

2. Describe the picture. How does it relate to the slogan *Not every cable channel is everyone's cup of tea*?

3. *Point* means "main idea." Explain the statement *That's the whole point.*

© 1992 Hershey Foods Corporation

How to help a clam come out of its shell.

Tempt it with white wine. Cajole it with garlic. Shock it with a pinch of red pepper. With encouragement like this, a clam can't help but open up. And that's when it's time to open up the Ronzoni. May we suggest our Angel Hair. This fine pasta is so delicately textured, it lets the clam's own subtle flavor come through. In fact, whether you make this light sauce or a zesty meat sauce, there's a pasta that's perfect, because Ronzoni makes over 50 kinds. So open up a box of Ronzoni. You'll be happy as a clam.

RONZONI
The Premium Pasta Maker

Angel Hair Pasta with Garlic and Clams

36 small fresh clams, scrubbed
3 tablespoons butter or margarine
3 tablespoons olive or vegetable oil
2 cloves garlic, minced

1-3/4 cups bottled clam juice
1/3 cup dry white wine or chicken broth
1-1/2 teaspoons dried oregano leaves

1/4 teaspoon crushed dried red pepper
1 pkg. (12 oz.) RONZONI Angel Hair pasta, uncooked
1/2 cup chopped fresh parsley

In large saucepan, add clams and about 3/4 cup water. Boil, covered, until clams open, about 5 minutes; discard clams that do not open. Remove clams from shells; chop coarsely and set aside. In large skillet, heat butter and oil. Add garlic; cook 1 minute. Add clam juice, wine, oregano and pepper. Boil uncovered, until liquid is reduced by half; about 10 minutes. Cook pasta according to package directions; drain. Add parsley and clams to sauce. Pour sauce over pasta; toss. 4 servings. Or substitute 1 can (6-1/2 oz.) chopped clams, drained.

1. The idiom *open up* means "to begin to talk." According to the ad, *a clam can't help but open up* when you add white wine, garlic, or red pepper. Explain how this idea relates to the slogan *How to help a clam come out of its shell.*

2. The idiom *happy as a clam* means "very happy." Explain the connection between the statement *You'll be happy as a clam* at the end of the ad and the other two idioms in this ad.

Reprinted with the permission of New World Pasta.

THINKING ABOUT THE ADS

Review the ads in this chapter. Choose the one that you like best. Complete the following statements based on that ad.

1. The ad that I like the best is . . . because . . . .

2. I think Americans would like this ad because . . . .

3. It is important to many Americans to . . . .

4. Other examples in American life that show how Americans feel about this value are . . . .

5. People from my country would/would not like this ad because . . . .

III Using the Idioms

USING THE IDIOMS IN SPEECH

A. Name That Idiom!

Play the following game in pairs. Try to be the first pair in your class to finish.

1. With a partner, copy the idioms from the list on page 29 onto separate index cards.

2. Divide the cards into two piles. Give one pile to your partner. Do not look at each other's cards.

3. Choose one card from your pile. Give a definition of the idiom or a sentence that illustrates its meaning <u>without</u> using the idiom.

4. After identifying the idiom correctly, your partner chooses a card from his or her pile and gives a definition or sentence.

5. Continue back and forth until you and your partner have correctly guessed all the idioms.

B. Round-Robin Story

Complete the following story in small groups.

1. One student adds to the story that begins below, using one of the idioms from this chapter.

2. The next student continues the story, using another idiom from this chapter.

3. Continue until all the idioms have been used and the story has ended.

   Susan was a sweet, quiet girl who was going to be married on Sunday to Fred Hawthorne. She probably would have gotten married and lived a nice, quiet life, but on Friday morning Susan met Benjamin. The first time she saw him, she knew she had to find out what made him tick. . . .

C. Role Play

Perform a role play in pairs.

1. Imagine that you are one of the characters at the top of page 42. You may refer to the script of *The Matchmaking Game* on page 32 for background information.

2. Write a script for a role play. Use as many of the idioms from this chapter as you can.

3. Practice the role play.

4. Perform the role play for your classmates.

THOMAS: You are Bachelor Number 2. You are on your first date with Vivian, and you're glad she chose you. You hope you can spend more time with her. Ask her about herself.

VIVIAN: You are on your first date with Thomas. The date is going well, and you're very impressed with him. You're glad you chose him on *The Matchmaking Game*. Ask him about himself.

USING THE IDIOMS IN WRITING

D. Writing with Idioms

Write a personal ad.

Describe yourself. Then describe what you are looking for in a companion. Use at least two idioms from this chapter in your ad.

E. Advertising with Idioms

Create an ad for a product or service.

1. Choose a product or service that you would like to advertise.

2. Determine your audience—the people most likely to buy your product or service.

3. Write a slogan for your ad, using one or more of the idioms from this chapter.

4. Decide on what picture(s) you will use in your ad.

5. Write the rest of your ad.

6. Present your ad to the class. Do your classmates understand your use of the idiom? Would they buy your product or service?

REVIEW I

Chapters 1–3

I. Which One Does Not Belong?

Read the situations below. Each situation can be completed with <u>two</u> of the three choices. Cross out the choice that is <u>not</u> correct.

1. Patty practices the piano two hours a day. Playing in the concert was
    a. a breeze.
    b. ~~not her cup of tea.~~
    c. a piece of cake.

2. Mr. Jones hired Tom to mow the lawn. When Tom was finished, Mr. Jones noticed that the edge of the grass was not cut well. However, he didn't say anything to Tom.
    a. Tom went out of his way to do a good job.
    b. Mr. Jones decided to lighten up about Tom's work.
    c. Mr. Jones left well enough alone.

3. Julianne and her friends were planning to go to a rock concert. She was very angry to learn that the tickets were sold out.
    a. She was up in arms over the tickets.
    b. She was counting on going to the concert.
    c. The concert knocked her socks off.

4. Jerry enjoys spending Sundays watching football on TV with his friends.
    a. On Sundays, Jerry hangs out with his friends.
    b. Sometimes Jerry is a couch potato.
    c. Jerry sees red when he watches football.

5. Felicia was trying to lose weight, so
    a. she ate salads, although they weren't her cup of tea.
    b. she didn't turn down candy or cake.
    c. she tried to kick the habit of eating between meals.

II. Describing People

Write a short paragraph describing each of the people pictured below. Use the idioms provided.

1. green thumb, a piece of cake

2. see red, work oneself into a lather

3. up in arms, leave well enough alone

4. do something for a living, count on someone

5. to each his own, what makes someone tick

6. turn down, not one's cup of tea

Chapter 4

RESOLUTIONS

Idioms

GET THE LEAD OUT

GO WITH THE FLOW

HAVE TIME ON ONE'S HANDS

ON A ROLL

RUN LATE

STAY ON TRACK

TAKE SOMETHING LIGHTLY

UP TO SOMEONE

AeroMexico Airlines

I Learning the Idioms

WARMING UP

Complete the following activities in pairs or small groups. Compare answers and discuss with your classmates.

1. At the beginning of a new year, people often make New Year's resolutions, or promises to themselves, to change their behavior or habits. For example, popular New Year's resolutions include exercising more, meeting new people, or learning a new skill.

   • On your own, write a list of five resolutions for the next year. These can include goals related to health, education, or any other area of your life.

   • Discuss your resolutions. Which will be easy to achieve? Why? Which will be difficult?

2. People who achieve their resolutions usually plan ahead.

   • As a class, choose a resolution. Possible resolutions include:

improve your health	improve your English
learn to play an instrument	travel around the world
become rich	win a cooking contest
lose weight	make more friends

   • In small groups, spend three minutes brainstorming different ways to achieve the resolution. Write them down.

   • Share your ideas with the class. The group with the most ideas is the winner.

3. Have you ever made a New Year's resolution? If so, what did you promise to do? Did you keep your resolution? Explain.

GETTING TO KNOW THE IDIOMS

A. Listening for Understanding

Listen to the man's speech about his New Year's resolutions. Think about the following questions. Then discuss your answers in pairs or small groups.

1. At the beginning, does the man seem likely to accomplish his goals? Why or why not?

2. What goals does he set about being punctual?

3. What does he say he will do with any extra time he has?

4. What does he say about diet and exercise?

5. Do you think he will accomplish his goals? Why or why not?

B. Identifying the Idioms

The idioms listed below are used throughout the speech you just heard. Read the script of the recording on page 48. Underline the idioms. Number them on the list below in the order they occur. Try to guess the meaning of each idiom by looking at how it is used.

____ get the lead out   ____ run late

____ go with the flow   ____ stay on track

____ have time on one's hands   ____ take something lightly

____ on a roll   ____ up to someone

New Year's Resolutions

New Year's resolutions. Everybody makes them. Everybody breaks them. But this time it'll be different. This year I'm very serious about my goals. I'm not going to take my resolutions lightly. I'm going to be determined! I'm going to be strong! If I say I'm going to do something, I'll do it! Next year, I'll be a different person. You'll see.

This time I won't forget all about my resolutions in another week or two. Really! This year I'm going to stay on track. I'm going to succeed. Others may not believe that I can do it, but I'll prove them wrong. You'll see.

This year I'm always going to be punctual. No more running late—to work, to appointments, to catch the bus. I'm going to get the lead out and move faster. You'll see.

And that's not all. This year I'm going to read more and watch TV less. When I have time on my hands, I'll study a foreign language or read the dictionary. I'll take violin lessons. I'll learn how to cook Italian food. You'll see.

This year I'll lose ten pounds. I'll exercise every day. I'll learn how to ski and roller skate and surf. I'm on a roll now! I'll hike up mountains. I'll learn how to scuba dive and fly an airplane. You'll see!

This year things are going to change. I won't be like everybody else. I won't just go with the flow. I'm going to be different! I'm going to make something of myself. You'll see.

It's all up to me! I can change my life, and I'm going to do it . . . right after I take a long nap. You know, all these resolutions have made me tired. But after my nap . . . well, you'll see.

C.   Getting the Meaning

Look at the underlined phrase in each of the following statements. Pay attention to how the idiom is used, and try to guess its meaning. You may also refer to the script of New Year's Resolutions *on page 48. Choose from the definitions below. Write the letter on the line.*

___h___   1. Do you want to go to the mountains or the coast this weekend? It's <u>up to you</u>.

_____   2. Mac and I run together, but he runs much faster than I do. He's always telling me to <u>get the lead out</u>.

_____   3. Marilyn stopped practicing the violin for a few months. However, she has <u>stayed on track</u> for the past four weeks.

_____   4. My doctor's appointment is at 10:00, but I'm <u>running late</u>.

_____   5. Mr. Brady <u>took his doctor's advice lightly</u>. Therefore, he didn't get better.

_____   6. Manny didn't want to stop gambling that night because he was <u>on a roll</u>.

_____   7. Thomas and Wendy are very different. Thomas tries to control every situation, but Wendy prefers to <u>go with the flow</u>.

_____   8. On Saturday I <u>had some time on my hands</u>, so I went for a long walk.

a. to accept a situation without trying to change it

b. delayed; likely to arrive or finish after the scheduled time

c. having repeated success

d. to be less serious than one should be about something

e. to work harder or move faster

f. to have extra, unscheduled time

g. to do something repeatedly and consistently

h. someone's decision or choice

PRACTICING THE IDIOMS

D.   Choosing the Best Answer

Listen to each short conversation. Then listen to the statement that follows. Circle T *if the statement is true and* F *if it is false.*

1. Ⓣ/ F   2. T / F   3. T / F   4. T / F

5. T / F   6. T / F   7. T / F   8. T / F

E. Retelling the Story

Read the script of New Year's Resolutions *on page 48 again. The sentences below refer to statements in that script. Restate the sentences, using the appropriate idioms. Try to write them* <u>without</u> *looking at the script again.*

1. This year I will be very serious about my resolutions.

   This year I will not take my resolutions lightly.

2. This time I will continue doing what I have resolved to do.

   _____

3. This year I'm not going to be late for everything.

   _____

4. I'm going to work harder and go faster.

   _____

5. If I have extra time, I'll study a foreign language or read the dictionary.

   _____

6. This year I'll learn to ski, roller skate, and surf. And I have even more plans!

   _____

7. I won't just accept every situation.

   _____

8. Changing my life is my decision.

   _____

F. Putting the Idioms into Practice

Maggie is meeting with her professor, Dr. Jones. Read their conversation. Circle the idiom that completes each sentence correctly.

DR. JONES: Maggie, at the beginning of the year you had all A's. You were

(taking your grades lightly / on a roll). But now your grades in this class
1.

are terrible. I'll have to drop you from the class if things don't improve.

MAGGIE: Oh, Dr. Jones, please don't do that! I know I haven't been studying very

hard, but I'll change! I promise I won't (take it lightly / get the lead out)
2.

anymore.

DR. JONES: Well, it's (on a roll / up to you). But you're going to have to show me
3.

that you're serious about your grades. You'll also have to start getting to

class on time. It's important to be in your seat when class begins.

MAGGIE: You're right. I don't know why I always (run late / have time on my hands)
4.

in the morning.

DR. JONES: I know the class starts early, but you just have to wake up and

(go with the flow / get the lead out) in the morning.
5.

MAGGIE: I will do that, Dr. Jones. It's true that I would

(have more time on my hands / run late) if I got up earlier
6.

each day. Then I would get here sooner.

DR. JONES: Maggie, I enjoy having you in my class. I want you to do well,

but your behavior will have to change. You can't just

(stay on track / go with the flow) and expect to succeed.
7.

MAGGIE: Dr. Jones, starting tomorrow, I'll be your best student. I'll

(stay on track / take things lightly) and start getting A's again. I won't
8.

disappoint you.

DR. JONES: OK, Maggie. I hope so!

II Finding the Idioms in Ads

INTERPRETING THE ADS

Look at the following ads. Determine what is being advertised. Find the featured idiom in each ad and review its meaning. Then answer the questions.

GO WITH THE FLOW.

OR

GO WITH THE FUTURE.

Follow or lead. Be someone's assistant or someone's role model. It's your choice. Teach For America is the national teacher corps of recent college graduates from a diversity of backgrounds and academic majors who commit two years to teach in urban and rural public schools. For an application or more information call 1 800 832-1230.

TEACH FOR AMERICA Ⓐ
A member of the AmeriCorps National Service Network

TWO YEARS. YOUR LIFE. OUR FUTURE.

Reprinted with the permission of Teach for America.

1. Describe the picture. What jobs do you think the people on the left have? What job do you think the man on the right has? Which job looks more interesting?

2. How does the statement *Go with the flow* relate to the people on the left?

3. Explain the statement *Go with the future*. How does it relate to the man on the right?

4. This ad is for a program called Teach for America that encourages college graduates to teach in public schools for two years. Do you think this is a good idea? Why or why not?

1. 3M is the company that makes *Scotch tape*. What is Scotch tape?

2. Scotch tape is sold by the *roll*. Explain two meanings of the statement *We've been on a roll for 67 years.*

3. The literal meaning of *pop up* is "to come out suddenly and easily." The idiomatic meaning is "to suddenly think of." Find one literal use and one idiomatic use in the ad.

Reprinted with the permission of 3M.

Reprinted with the permission of American Designer Pottery.

1. Describe the picture.

2. Is pottery usually light or heavy? Do you think the pottery in the picture is light or heavy? Why?

3. Do you think the woman in the picture usually *takes things lightly*? Why?

4. Is the phrase *taken . . . lightly* in the slogan *Never before has fine pottery been taken so lightly* used literally, idiomatically, or both ways? Explain.

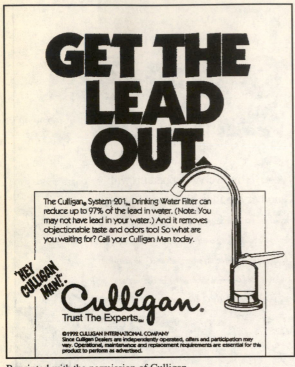

Reprinted with the permission of Culligan.

1. Some drinking water contains lead, which is a very harmful substance. Culligan sells a water purification system. What claims does Culligan make about its system?

2. Is the phrase *get the lead out* used literally, idiomatically, or both ways? Explain.

1. Describe the picture. What is the man doing? Where do you think he's going?

2. AeroMexico claims to be the world's most punctual airline. Explain the slogan *If you're running late, don't bother coming.*

3. How is the picture related to the slogan?

AeroMexico Airlines

1. *Hand washables* are clothes that should be washed by hand, not in a washing machine. According to this ad, what should you do with hand washables?

2. How will using this washing machine give you more *time on your hands*?

3. *Suds* are bubbles made from using soap. Explain the statement *For it's nicer to have time on your hands than suds.*

Leave your hand washables to the *Ultimate Care™ System.*
For it's nicer to have time on your hands than suds.

"Hand Wash Only"? Nah...just toss it in. Our Ultimate Care two-speed washers have an exclusive pulse action switch, which turns the agitator on and off during the cycle. This, combined with a slow agitation, cleans your hand washables the gentlest way

possible. Plus, some Whirlpool® models offer the AccuWash Sensor,™ which monitors water temperature to help control shrinking. So visit www.whirlpool.com or call 1-800-253-1301. And free your hands up for something more fun.

Whirlpool
A Job Well Done.™

Reprinted with the permission of Whirlpool Corporation.

THINKING ABOUT THE ADS

Review the ads in this chapter. Choose the one that you like best. Complete the following statements based on that ad.

1. The ad that I like the best is . . . because . . . .

2. I think Americans would like this ad because . . . .

3. It is important to many Americans to . . . .

4. Other examples in American life that show how Americans feel about this value are . . . .

5. People from my country would/would not like this ad because . . . .

III Using the Idioms

USING THE IDIOMS IN SPEECH

A. Name That Idiom!

Play the following game in pairs. Try to be the first pair in your class to finish.

1. With a partner, copy the idioms from the list on page 46 onto separate index cards.

2. Divide the cards into two piles. Give one pile to your partner. Do not look at each other's cards.

3. Choose one card from your pile. Give a definition of the idiom or a sentence that illustrates its meaning <u>without</u> using the idiom.

4. After identifying the idiom correctly, your partner chooses a card from his or her pile and gives a definition or sentence.

5. Continue back and forth until you and your partner have correctly guessed all the idioms.

B. Round-Robin Story

Complete the following story in small groups.

1. One student adds to the story that begins below, using one of the idioms from this chapter.

2. The next student continues the story, using another idiom from this chapter.

3. Continue until all the idioms have been used and the story has ended.

As a teenager, Lena never said much. If her friends wanted to go see a movie that she had already seen, she would go with the flow and see it again. Her friends were sure that she had no personal opinions about anything.

Twenty years later, Lena met one of her old friends, Pauline, on the street. Pauline was very surprised. Lena seemed to be a completely different person . . . .

C.　Role Play

Perform a role play in pairs.

1. Imagine that you are one of the characters below. You may refer to the script of *New Year's Resolutions* on page 48 for background information.

2. Write a script for a role play. Use as many of the idioms from this chapter as you can.

3. Practice the role play.

4. Perform the role play for your classmates.

JESS:　　You have just finished writing your New Year's resolutions. This year you are determined to change your life. You are going to lose weight, learn a new skill, and study harder. Tell your friend Sophie about your goals.

SOPHIE:　Your friend Jess has never been very responsible. He doesn't work very hard, and he usually lets others make decisions for him. You're surprised that he seems so serious about his New Year's resolutions, and you don't think that he'll be able to keep them. Try to persuade him to be more realistic about his goals.

USING THE IDIOMS IN WRITING

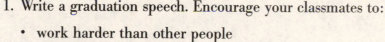

D.　Writing with Idioms

Imagine that you are the valedictorian[1] for your high school class.

1. Write a graduation speech. Encourage your classmates to:

   * work harder than other people
   * do their best
   * be serious about the future
   * be on time for job interviews or classes
   * make their own decisions

   Use at least four of the idioms from this chapter.

2. Be prepared to give the speech in class.

---

[1]top student in a graduating class, who gives a speech at graduation

E.   Advertising with Idioms

Create an ad for a product or service.

1. Choose a product or service that you would like to advertise.

2. Determine your audience—the people most likely to buy your product or service.

3. Write a slogan for your ad, using one or more of the idioms from this chapter.

4. Decide on what picture(s) you will use in your ad.

5. Write the rest of your ad.

6. Present your ad to the class. Do your classmates understand your use of the idiom? Would they buy your product or service?

Chapter **5**

CRIME

Idioms

BEG TO DIFFER

GET SOMETHING

GET TO THE BOTTOM OF SOMETHING

HAND IT TO SOMEONE

ON EASY STREET

PAY THE PRICE

PULL THE WOOL OVER SOMEONE'S EYES

SEE RIGHT THROUGH SOMEONE OR SOMETHING

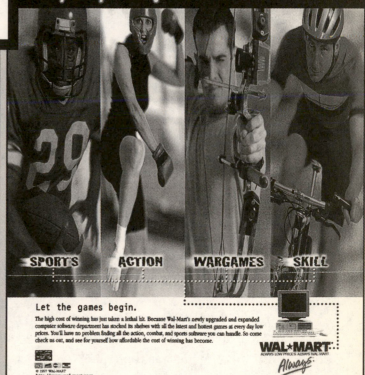

Reprinted with the permission of Wal-Mart stores.

I Learning the Idioms

WARMING UP

Complete the following activities in pairs or small groups. Compare answers and discuss with your classmates.

1. Have you heard about a famous crime? If so, describe it. Answer the following questions.
   - What was the crime?
   - In what country was the crime committed?
   - Who was the criminal?
   - Who was the victim?
   - What was the motive (reason) for the crime?

2. A crime has been committed. The items and people in the pictures below were involved in the crime.

As a group, create a story about the crime. Include as many of the items and people from the pictures as you can. Be sure to answer the following questions.

What was the crime?	Who was the victim?
Who was the criminal?	What was the motive?

There is no "right" answer. Many stories are possible.

Share your story with the rest of the class.

GETTING TO KNOW THE IDIOMS

A. Listening for Understanding

Listen to the conversation between a detective and a suspect.[1] Think about the following questions. Also, try to guess how the detective solved the crime. Then discuss your answers in pairs or small groups.

1. Who is Mr. Johnson? Who is Cameron Smithers? What kind of relationship do they have?

2. Which man was missing? What happened to him?

3. Why was Cameron angry with Mr. Johnson?

4. Why do you think Cameron killed Mr. Johnson?

5. How did Detective Moore know he did it?

6. What do you think will happen next?

B. Identifying the Idioms

The idioms listed below are used throughout the conversation you just heard. Read the script of the conversation on page 62. Underline the idioms. Number them on the list below in the order they occur. Try to guess the meaning of each idiom by looking at how it is used.

____ beg to differ

____ get something

____ get to the bottom of something

____ hand it to someone

____ on Easy Street

____ pay the price

____ pull the wool over someone's eyes

____ see right through someone or something

---
[1] person who may have committed a crime

A Murder Mystery

Mr. Johnson hired Cameron Smithers to work in his store. Cameron was a good worker, but soon Mr. Johnson began to suspect that Cameron was stealing from him. Sometime later, Mr. Johnson was found dead in his home. Detective Moore is asking Cameron some questions.

MOORE: Good afternoon, Cameron. Your boss, Mr. Johnson, is missing. Do you know where he is?

CAMERON: No. I quit my job last week, so I haven't been to work.

MOORE: When was the last time you saw Mr. Johnson?

CAMERON: Friday afternoon. He said that he was missing some money and that he was going to get to the bottom of it. He told me he was going to call the police to investigate.

MOORE: Then what happened? You must have been very angry.

CAMERON: Of course I was angry! I just don't get it! I always worked hard for him. I told him I was going to quit, and then I left the store.

MOORE: Did you think he should pay you more?

CAMERON: Sure! Mr. Johnson was rich. Everyone knows he was living on Easy Street.

MOORE: Did you want to kill him?

CAMERON: No! I don't know how he died.

MOORE: I beg to differ, Cameron. I believe you killed him so he couldn't report you to the police. You were stealing from him, and he knew it. You didn't want anyone else to find out. Isn't that right?

CAMERON: Of course not!

MOORE: Don't try to pull the wool over my eyes, Cameron. Why don't you admit that you killed him!

CAMERON: No! I was at home on Friday night. I never even went to his house!

MOORE: Cameron, I can see right through your alibi. Now I have proof that you were the one. This time you're going to pay the price for your crime. You're going to prison!

CAMERON: Well, Detective Moore, I've got to hand it to you. How did you figure it out so fast?

C. Getting the Meaning

Look at the underlined phrase in each of the following statements. Pay attention to how the idiom is used, and try to guess its meaning. You may also refer to the script of A Murder Mystery on page 62. Choose from the definitions below. Write the letter on the line.

  _b_   1. Carl just told a joke, but I didn't <u>get it</u>.

  ____   2. Carol stole the money, but she tried to <u>pull the wool over my eyes</u> by blaming it on John.

  ____   3. I don't understand this problem now, but I'll <u>get to the bottom of it</u> soon.

  ____   4. Many professional athletes make so much money that they're <u>on Easy Street</u> for the rest of their lives.

  ____   5. "I think that Fred Everett would be the best president for our club." "<u>I beg to differ</u>. Melanie Wilson is much better qualified."

  ____   6. Marvin drank too much beer last night, so today he has to <u>pay the price</u>. He's been sick all morning.

  ____   7. Clark pretends to be interested in the project, but I can <u>see right through him</u>. He really doesn't care.

  ____   8. I've got to <u>hand it to Ms. Norwood</u>. After a lot of hard work, she finally won the prize

a. to disagree

b. to understand something

c. to discover the reason for something

d. in a worry-free state (especially about money)

e. to be punished; to suffer the consequences

f. to trick or deceive someone

g. to give someone credit for something

h. to know the truth in spite of outward appearances; to recognize falseness

PRACTICING THE IDIOMS

D. Choosing the Best Answer

Listen to the statements. Read the sentences below. Circle T *if the sentence is true and* F *if it is false.*

1. T /Ⓕ   I have to pay for the test.

2. T / F   My boyfriend didn't plan anything for my birthday.

3. T / F   The money was in the bottom of the drawer.

4. T / F   I'll be very rich if I'm the winner.

5. T / F   Mrs. Stallings doesn't care about poor people.

6. T / F   My grandmother knows how to dye people's hair.

7. T / F   Joe and I both like Burger Barn's hamburgers best.

8. T / F   Marian won the chess game.

E. Retelling the Story

Read the script of A Murder Mystery *on page 62 again. The sentences below refer to statements in that script. Restate the sentences, using the appropriate idioms. Try to write them* underline{without} *looking at the script again.*

1. Mr. Johnson said he would discover the reason the money was missing.

     Mr. Johnson said he would get to the bottom of the missing money.

2. Cameron said he didn't understand Mr. Johnson's actions.

     _____

3. Mr. Johnson never had to worry about money.

     _____

4. Detective Moore said he disagreed with Cameron.

     _____

5. Detective Moore told Cameron not to try to deceive him.

     _____

6. Detective Moore could see the falseness of Cameron's statements.

     _____

7. Detective Moore told Cameron that he would have to be punished for his crime.

     _____

8. Cameron gave credit to Detective Moore for solving the crime so quickly.

     _____

F. Putting the Idioms into Practice

Read the paragraph below. Then read the incomplete statements that follow. Choose the ending that completes each statement correctly. Circle a or b.

A man wanted to make a lot of money, so he decided to become a thief. His parents had always told him that the best way to get rich is to work hard, but he disagreed. He was lazy and didn't like to work, so he decided to steal a famous painting from a museum. The man was sure that he could sell the painting and never have to worry about money again. He quietly entered the museum and took the painting off the wall. However, just as he was carrying the picture away, a security guard arrived. The man tried to trick the guard by telling her that the painting needed repair. The guard inspected the painting and knew the man was lying. She couldn't understand why the man was trying to steal such a famous painting, since he would be punished for his crime. The next day, the museum director gave the guard full credit for saving the painting. The guard received a large reward for catching the thief.

1. The man's parents thought that he should work hard, but the man
   a. begged to differ.
   b. was on Easy Street.

2. The thief believed that after he sold the painting,
   a. he would be on Easy Street.
   b. he could hand it to someone.

3. The thief
   a. saw right through the security guard.
   b. tried to pull the wool over the guard's eyes.

4. The guard
   a. could see right through the thief's lies.
   b. had to hand it to the thief.

5. The security guard quickly
   a. paid the price for catching the thief.
   b. got to the bottom of things.

6. It seemed strange that the thief would steal that painting. The security guard
   a. didn't get it.
   b. pulled the wool over the thief's eyes.

7. The thief
   a. had to pay the price for his crime.
   b. begged to differ with the guard.

8. Because the security guard did such a good job, the museum director
   a. got to the bottom of the case.
   b. had to hand it to her.

II Finding the Idioms in Ads

INTERPRETING THE ADS

Look at the following ads. Determine what is being advertised. Find the featured idiom in each ad and review its meaning. Then answer the questions.

FOR $48 YOU CAN PULL THE WOOL OVER HIS EYES.

He'll think his new Aran sweater costs hundreds of dollars. But for only $48 you'll receive our Worsted Weight Easy Knit Pattern, sizes 3 and 6 needles, plus ample wool to knit this beautiful sweater.

The pattern is for male and female so you can pull the wool over your eyes too. (Smaller sizes only cost $39.)

QUALITY WOOL. The wool is a traditional crepe yarn of 100% Australian wool in 200g skeins. The quality of this yarn is guaranteed by Bendigo Woollen Mills.

ORDERING IS SIMPLE. Just choose your Size* and preferred Color on the coupon below and mail to: Bendigo Woollen Mills Pty Ltd.
P.O. Box 27164, Columbus, Ohio 43227
Phone 1-800-829 WOOL where your order will be promptly shipped.

BENDIGO WOOLLEN MILLS

NB. The printing process does not permit exact color reproduction. Colors will vary slightly in appearance.

Shade	Colour	Small @ $39.00*	Large @ $48.00*	Price
Mallard				
Red				
Jade				
Black				
Amethyst				
Camelia				
Navy				
Dusty Blue				
Magnolia				
Nut Brown				
Rust				
Olive				

*Small Sizes 32", 34" & 36" @ $39.00
*Large Sizes 38", 40" & 42" @ $48.00

TOTAL $

Mr/Mrs/Miss/Ms _____
Address _____
State _____ Zipcode _____ Tel No. _____
Payment Method ☐Check ☐M/Order ☐Mastercard ☐Visa
Card No. _____
Exp. Date _____ Signature _____

FREE SHADE CARD. Send for our free shade card for a complete range of yarns and shades.

Reprinted with the permission of Bendigo Woollen Mills.

1. What is this sweater made of?

2. What do you get if you send in the order form?

3. According to the ad, the sweater looks like it costs hundreds of dollars. If you make this sweater for only $48, how can you *pull the wool over someone's eyes*?

1. *Wheels* is slang for "a car." What kind of car would someone *on Easy Street* drive?

2. What is pictured in the ad? What are the wheels used for?

3. Who is the audience for this ad? How can these wheels make their lives easier?

The wheels seen most often on Easy Street.

For the discriminating traveler, Lark® introduces a luxury vehicle with superior handling. 1994's Lark Permaflex E-Z Wheeler.® It's built-in Piggyback® system can comfortably seat another bag, while the sturdy wide-track wheels make every trip a Sunday drive. And its unique Permaflex shell combines the protection of a hard-side suitcase with the lightweight feel of a softside. Lark makes it a joy to be on the road. For more information and your nearest showroom, call 1-800-421-LARK.

Reserved For Those Who Have Earned Their Stripes.℠

Reprinted with the permission of Samsonite.

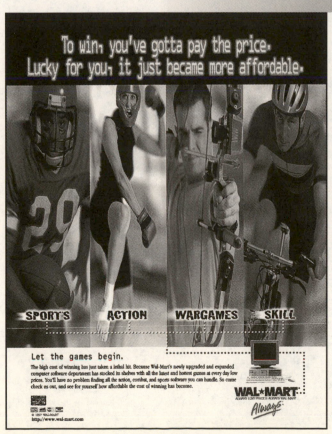

To win, you've gotta pay the price. Lucky for you, it just became more affordable.

SPORTS   ACTION   WARGAMES   SKILL

Let the games begin.

The high cost of winning has just taken a lethal hit. Because Wal-Mart's newly upgraded and expanded computer software department has stocked its shelves with all the latest and hottest games at every day low prices. You'll have no problem finding all the action, combat, and sports software you can handle. So come check us out, and see for yourself how affordable the cost of winning has become.

© 1997 WAL-MART
http://www.wal-mart.com

WAL★MART
ALWAYS LOW PRICES. ALWAYS WAL-MART
Always

Reprinted with the permission of Wal-Mart stores.

1. What games are pictured in the ad? To win at them, what do you have to do?

2. This company claims to have very low prices. How does that claim relate to the phrase *pay the price*?

3. *Gotta* is short for "got to." Explain the statement *To win, you've gotta pay the price.*

Heinz Pet Products™ is owned by StarKist Foods, Inc. and is used with permission.

1. How many different dog foods are pictured? Which one interests the dogs the most?

2. What do you think the dogs would say about the product?

3. Dogs often beg for food by standing on their back legs. Explain the two meanings of the statement *Dogs beg to differ.*

1. A *compartment* is a small enclosed space inside a larger space. What compartments are there in a car?

2. Describe the picture. What items are on the left? Where do the broken lines indicate they should be placed?

3. Explain the slogan *You've got to hand it to our engineers in the compartment department.* What did the engineers do?

Courtesy of the Dodge Division of the Daimler Chrysler Corporation.

1. Who is Cinderella? Tell her story.

2. What kind of shoes did Cinderella wear to the prince's ball? How do these shoes relate to the expression *see right through something*?

3. The proverb *If the shoe fits, wear it* means that if a description about you is true, you should accept it. (Example: *"Are you saying that I'm rude?" "If the shoe fits, wear it."*) What product is being advertised? Explain the statement *The shoe fits. Wear it.*

Rosetta ETS for aerobics

*J*f Cinderella had known about RYKÄ ETS, she would have seen right through the glass slipper.

The shoe fits. Wear it.

RYKÄ
exclusively for women

To find out about ETS call toll free 888-834-RYKA

RYKÄ

THINKING ABOUT THE ADS

Review the ads in this chapter. Choose the one that you like best. Complete the following statements based on that ad.

1. The ad that I like the best is . . . because . . . .

2. I think Americans would like this ad because . . . .

3. It is important to many Americans to . . . .

4. Other examples in American life that show how Americans feel about this value are . . . .

5. People from my country would/would not like this ad because . . . .

III Using the Idioms

USING THE IDIOMS IN SPEECH

A. Name That Idiom!

Play the following game in pairs. Try to be the first pair in your class to finish.

1. With a partner, copy the idioms from the list on page 59 onto separate index cards.

2. Divide the cards into two piles. Give one pile to your partner. Do not look at each other's cards.

3. Choose one card from your pile. Give a definition of the idiom or a sentence that illustrates its meaning <u>without</u> using the idiom.

4. After identifying the idiom correctly, your partner chooses a card from his or her pile and gives a definition or sentence.

5. Continue back and forth until you and your partner have correctly guessed all the idioms.

B. Round-Robin Story

Complete the following story in small groups.

1. One student adds to the story that begins below, using one of the idioms from this chapter.

2. The next student continues the story, using another idiom from this chapter.

3. Continue until all the idioms have been used and the story has ended.

One morning this headline appeared in the newspaper: BOY LIVING ON EASY STREET AFTER FINDING BURIED TREASURE! . . .

C. Role Play

Perform a role play in pairs.

1. Imagine that you are one of the characters below. You may refer to the script of *A Murder Mystery* on page 62 for background information.

2. Write a script for a role play. Use as many of the idioms from this chapter as you can.

3. Practice the role play.

4. Perform the role play for your classmates.

CAMERON: You are angry because your boss, Mr. Johnson, is very rich and you don't think he pays you enough. You think Mr. Johnson should be punished for his selfishness. Tell him that you have been working hard and that you think you deserve more.

MR. JOHNSON: You think that Cameron has been stealing from you. He has tried to deceive you many times before, but you know when he is lying. Tell him that you're going to prove he has been stealing the money and that he will be punished for it.

USING THE IDIOMS IN WRITING

D. Writing with Idioms

Imagine that you are a newspaper reporter.

Write a newspaper report about this picture. Be sure to answer the following questions.

- Who was trying to steal the jewels?

- Why did he want to steal them?

- How did the police officer catch him?

- What did the burglar tell the police officer after he was caught?

- What did the policeman say to him?

Use at least four idioms from this chapter in your report.

E. Advertising with Idioms

Create an ad for a product or service.

1. Choose a product or service that you would like to advertise.

2. Determine your audience—the people most likely to buy your product or service.

3. Write a slogan for your ad, using one or more of the idioms from this chapter.

4. Decide on what picture(s) you will use in your ad.

5. Write the rest of your ad.

6. Present your ad to the class. Do your classmates understand your use of the idiom? Would they buy your product or service?

Chapter 6

STRANGE STORIES

Idioms

CREATE A STIR

EAT ONE'S WORDS

IN A JAM

MAKE FUN OF SOMEONE OR SOMETHING

OUT OF THE BLUE

PLAY WITH FIRE

TAKE SOMEONE OR SOMETHING SERIOUSLY

THROW CAUTION TO THE WIND

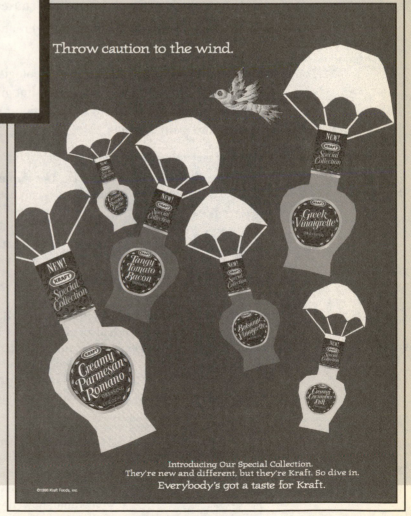

Reprinted with permission of Kraft Foods, Inc.

I Learning the Idioms

WARMING UP

Complete the following activities in pairs or small groups. Compare answers and discuss with your classmates.

1. Many countries have legends about creatures whose existence cannot be proven. Examples of such creatures include Bigfoot (or Sasquatch) in North America, Yeti in the Himalayas, the Loch Ness monster in Scotland, and El Chupacabras (the Goatsucker) in Puerto Rico, Mexico, and Central America.

   • Have you heard about any of the legendary creatures above? If so, talk about what you know.

   • Do you believe that any of these creatures really exist? Why or why not?

   • If not, where do you think these stories come from?

   • Are there legends of any strange creatures in your country? If so, tell your classmates about them.

2. Imagine that you are a famous archeologist. You have an extraordinary opportunity. Adventure Time Travel, a company that gives tours of past civilizations, is offering the following trips into the past. Which one would you choose? Why? Discuss your choice and your reasons.

The Nasca Lines of Peru: Find out how the amazing and mysterious lines and figures of Nasca were made! These enormous markings form straight lines, geometric figures, and huge drawings of animals. But they can be seen only from the air! No one knows when or how or why they were made. This is your chance to find out!

The Great Pyramid of Egypt: Measurements of the Great Pyramid indicate that their builders had an extraordinary knowledge of the earth and the solar system. For example, the perimeter of the pyramid equals the number of days in a year. The height of the pyramid multiplied by 10^9 gives the distance from the earth to the sun. These and many more mathematical mysteries can be solved on this tour of the past!

Stonehenge in England: This ring of massive stones was probably built between 2800 and 1500 B.C. Most experts believe that the stones were used to determine when important astronomical events would occur. You can find out how this ancient civilization moved the huge stones and how they knew where to place them. Come see the beginnings of Stonehenge!

GETTING TO KNOW THE IDIOMS

A. Listening for Understanding

Listen to the report about the Bermuda Triangle. Think about the following questions. Then discuss your answers in pairs or small groups.

1. What happened to Christopher Columbus when he sailed through the area known as the Bermuda Triangle?

2. How many airplanes in Flight 19 disappeared? How many were later found?

3. What happened to the National Airlines flight that landed in Miami?

4. What was strange about the clocks and watches on board the airplane?

5. What do you think the best explanation is for the strange things that happen in the Bermuda Triangle?

6. Do you think the stories about people disappearing in the Bermuda Triangle are true? Why or why not?

7. Would *you* go on a cruise through the Bermuda Triangle? Why or why not?

B. Identifying the Idioms

The idioms listed below are used throughout the report you just heard. Read the script of the report on page 76. Underline the idioms. Number them on the list below in the order they occur. Try to guess the meaning of each idiom by looking at the words around it.

____ create a stir

____ eat one's words

____ in a jam

____ make fun of someone or something

____ out of the blue

____ play with fire

____ take someone or something seriously

____ throw caution to the wind

The Bermuda Triangle

In 1492, just before he reached land, Christopher Columbus wrote that strange things were happening at sea. His ship's compass wasn't working right, and there were mysterious lights over the ocean. Today, the area that Columbus sailed through is famous because of the hundreds of ships and airplanes that have been lost there. This part of the ocean, which stretches from Florida to Puerto Rico to Bermuda, is often called the Bermuda Triangle.

Among the stories that have created a stir is the disappearance of Flight 19. In Flight 19, there were five United States Navy airplanes that were on a short and easy training mission. After reporting that the compass on the airplane wasn't working properly, one of the pilots radioed that they were in a jam. There was something wrong with their position; they were lost. Then the airplanes just disappeared. A rescue airplane was sent out to bring them back, but something happened to that airplane as well. It disappeared along with the others. None of the planes or the twenty-seven men on board were ever found.

Another bizarre incident involved a National Airlines passenger flight. Not long before it was supposed to land at Miami International Airport, the flight disappeared from the airport's radar screens. For ten minutes, the airplane could not be found on radar. But the flight did arrive on schedule. When it landed, the pilot said that, out of the blue, a strange fog had appeared and surrounded them for ten minutes. Even stranger, all the clocks and watches of the passengers and crew were ten minutes slow!

What do you believe? Do you take the stories of airplanes and ships disappearing in the Bermuda Triangle seriously? Some people think that UFOs are responsible. Others say that there are dangerous forces in the Bermuda Triangle and that traveling in that area is playing with fire. Most experts make fun of these ideas, offering other explanations, such as bad weather or accidents. However, it is true that thousands of people have disappeared in the Bermuda Triangle. People who say they don't believe it often have to eat their words when they examine the evidence.

So . . . what about you? If someone offered you a cruise through the Bermuda Triangle, would you throw caution to the wind? Would you take a chance? Would you go?

C. Getting the Meaning

Look at the underlined phrase in each of the following statements. Pay attention to how the idiom is used, and try to guess its meaning. You may also refer to the script of the report on The Bermuda Triangle *on page 76. Choose from the definitions below. Write the letter on the line.*

_g_　　1. Poor Mary Lou! Everyone <u>made fun of her</u> when her dress tore during class.

____　2. Barbara borrowed her friend's laptop computer and then lost it. Now she's really <u>in a jam</u>.

____　3. The first time Brent went skiing, he <u>threw caution to the wind</u> and broke his leg.

____　4. I was driving along when, <u>out of the blue</u>, that car crashed into me!

____　5. I said Albert was a terrible tennis player. When he won the match, I had to <u>eat my words</u>.

____　6. The new solar-powered car is <u>creating a stir</u> in the automobile industry.

____　7. Riding a motorcycle without wearing a helmet is <u>playing with fire</u>.

____　8. Few people really <u>take</u> the idea of UFOs landing on earth <u>seriously</u>.

a. to become reckless; to not worry about danger

b. to admit that one said something wrong

c. in a difficult situation

d. to do something dangerous or risky

e. to cause a disturbance or excitement

f. to believe or accept something

g. to ridicule

h. unexpectedly

PRACTICING THE IDIOMS

D. Choosing the Best Answer

Listen to each short conversation. Read the sentences below. Choose the sentence that best matches the conversation you heard. Circle a *or* b.

1. (a.) Some of Catherine's classmates make fun of her.
   b. Some of Catherine's classmates have to eat their words.

2. a. Ed's jewelry came out of the blue.
   b. Ed is in a jam.

3. a. People who use the new product will be playing with fire.
   b. The new product will create a stir among people living in the desert.

4. a. Paul is throwing caution to the wind.
   b. Paul is getting out of a jam.

5. a. Mrs. Graham had to eat her words.
   b. Mrs. Graham's visit came out of the blue.

6. a. Karen's father had to eat his words.
   b. Karen's father took her writing seriously.

7. a. Warren didn't take the man seriously.
   b. The man quit his job out of the blue.

8. a. The police create a stir on holidays.
   b. Drinking and driving is playing with fire.

E. Retelling the Story

Read the script of The Bermuda Triangle *on page 76 again. The sentences below refer to statements in that script. Restate the sentences, using the appropriate idioms. Try to write them __without__ looking at the report again.*

1. One report that caused a big commotion was the disappearance of Flight 19.

   One story that created a stir was the disappearance of Flight 19.

2. A pilot sent the message that they were in trouble.

   _____

3. The pilot reported that suddenly a fog appeared and surrounded them for ten minutes.

   _____

4. Do you believe the strange reports about the Bermuda Triangle?

   _____

5. Some people say that going into the Bermuda Triangle is taking a dangerous risk.

   _____

6. Most experts laugh at these ideas.

   _____

7. People who say the stories of the Bermuda Triangle are false often must later admit they were wrong.

   _____

8. If someone offered you a cruise through the Bermuda Triangle, would you take a risk and go?

   _____

F.   Putting the Idioms into Practice

Read the story below. Replace each numbered phrase with the appropriate idiom from the list.

created a stir   out of the blue

get out of the jam   playing with fire

eat their words   threw caution to the wind

made fun of   took her seriously

All her life, Regina Martin wanted to be a race car driver. When she was only five years old, she told her parents that she was going to drive race cars when she grew up. As she was growing up, she never changed her mind, although many of her friends

_____made fun of_____ her. They wanted to be movie stars or doctors or
                1. ridiculed

teachers—"normal" occupations. Of course, no one ever _____
                                                            2. believed her

when she said that one day she would be famous. But Regina was determined to

succeed.

   Regina _____ when she won her very first race and
                3. caused a commotion

many of the races she entered afterward. It wasn't long before she truly was famous,

and when her friends read about her in the newspapers, they had to

_____. Although she was normally quiet and polite,
      4. admit they were wrong

when Regina got into a race car, she _____, racing
                                          5. was reckless

aggressively and often dangerously. She said she had to do that to win when competing

against the men, but many people predicted that she would have an accident soon.

They said that she was _____. But as long as she was the only
                          6. doing something dangerous

woman on the track, she had to prove that she was just as good as the men.

Regina's last race came just seven years after she won her first one. She was

coming around the track too fast, and she was ahead of the other drivers with one lap

remaining. Perhaps she didn't pay attention for just a few seconds, but

_____ another driver pulled ahead of her. Regina's car
　　　7. unexpectedly

skidded to avoid hitting him, and she lost control. Although she tried to continue, she

couldn't _____ she was in. Her car crashed into a wall and
　　　　　　8. get out of trouble

burst into flames. Although she survived, Regina was unable to race again. However,

she often said that she was very glad to have had those experiences. She did what she

had dreamed of doing as a child.

II Finding the Idioms in Ads

INTERPRETING THE ADS

Look at the following ads. Determine what is being advertised. Find the featured idiom in each ad and review its meaning. Then answer the questions.

Throw caution to the wind.

Introducing Our Special Collection.
They're new and different, but they're Kraft. So dive in.
Everybody's got a taste for Kraft.

©1998 Kraft Foods, Inc.

Reprinted with permission of Kraft Foods, Inc.

1. Describe the picture. What are the bottles of salad dressing doing? What is on top of the bottles?

2. Why was the slogan *Throw caution to the wind* used in this ad?

3. *Dive in* means "to begin an activity with enthusiasm." Explain the phrase *So dive in.*

Reprinted with permission of Almond Board of California.

1. In this dish, called *stir-fry*, vegetables are fried quickly in a pan with a little oil. Why is the idiom *create a stir* used in this ad?

2. The expression *stir (something) up* means "to deliberately cause trouble or excitement." According to the ad, *Nothing stirs up an appetite for vegetables like a few well-placed California almonds*. Explain this statement.

3. What is the message of this ad?

1. The ad calls this product *the power tool for stains*. What is being advertised?

2. If the jam in the picture spills on your clothes, how are you *in a jam*?

3. *Bread* is a slang expression for "money." Rephrase the slogan *Get out of a jam for less bread*.

Proctor & Gamble

1. What product is being advertised?

2. Is the idiom in the slogan *It makes fun of computers* used idiomatically, literally, or both ways?

3. What is the message of this ad?

IT MAKES FUN OF COMPUTERS.

Kids get a lot of laughs when they play with the Team Concepts™ Super Computer.™

It's fun for children to use, which is something you can't say about most other learning computers.

Our Super Computer™ is built on the idea that kids learn more when they enjoy what they're doing.

While your kids are "playing" with the Super Computer," they're not only learning basic computer skills, but also spelling, language skills, number

skills from basic addition to fractions, music, history, science, and geography. And it's the only children's computer that lets the child store information such as friends' names and numbers and has a "password" so no one else can access it. Because the Team Concepts™ Super Computer™ teaches computer skills as well as everything from math to music, your children will learn a lot. But the most important thing they'll learn is how much fun it is.

For further information call: 1-800-186-0888

TEAMCONCEPTS
Our team turns learning into fun.

© 1991 Isteq, Inc. A Subsidiary of Team Concepts Holdings Ltd.

Reprinted with the permission of Team Concepts.

If You Don't Have Insul-Safe III® Insulation In Your Attic, You Could Be Playing With Fire.

Home insulation materials are all the same, right? Don't bet your life on it.

For example, cellulose insulation is made from ground-up newspaper, so it's naturally flammable, and has to be treated with chemicals to retard flammability. But recent tests show these chemicals may lose their effectiveness in as little as a few years. Which means if you have cellulose insulation in your home, you could be living with a potential fire hazard.

That's why smart homeowners choose INSUL-SAFE III® Fiber Glass Blown-in Insulation from CertainTeed.

INSUL-SAFE III is inorganic. And naturally noncombustible–from the day it's installed and throughout the life of your home. Which makes it one of the safest, most effective insulating materials available. To find out what kind of insulation you have in your attic, or to have INSUL-SAFE III installed, check the Yellow Pages under "Insulation Contractor." Or call CertainTeed at 1-800-782-8777. After all, why play with fire, when you can play it safe?

CertainTeed
Fiber Glass Insulation

Reprinted with the permission of CertainTeed Corporation.

1. What product is being advertised? What does it do? Where is it used?

2. According to the ad, other kinds of insulation burn easily, but Insul-Safe III insulation does not. How does this relate to the idiom *play with fire*?

3. *Play it safe* means "to act in a safe manner." Explain the question *After all, why play with fire, when you can play it safe?* at the bottom of the ad.

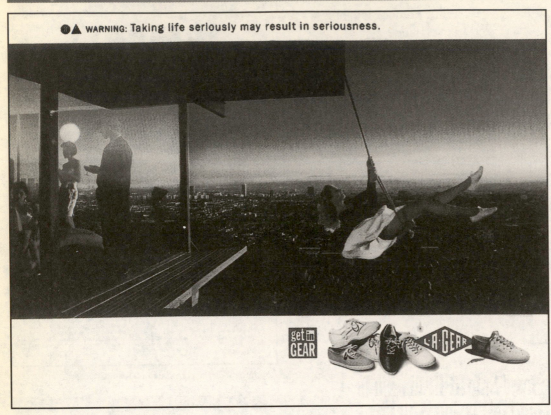

Reprinted with the permission of L.A. Gear.

1. Describe the picture. What are the people inside doing? What is the woman outside doing?

2. Who is taking life seriously? Who is having fun?

3. What product is being advertised?

4. What is the message of this ad?

THINKING ABOUT THE ADS

Review the ads in this chapter. Choose the one that you like best. Complete the following statements based on that ad.

1. The ad that I like the best is . . . because . . . .

2. I think Americans would like this ad because . . . .

3. It is important to many Americans to . . . .

4. Other examples in American life that show how Americans feel about this value are . . . .

5. People from my country would/would not like this ad because . . . .

III Using the Idioms

USING THE IDIOMS IN SPEECH

A. Name That Idiom!

Play the following game in pairs. Try to be the first pair in your class to finish.

1. With a partner, copy the idioms from the list on page 73 onto separate index cards.

2. Divide the cards into two piles. Give one pile to your partner. Do not look at each other's cards.

3. Choose one card from your pile. Give a definition of the idiom or a sentence that illustrates its meaning <u>without</u> using the idiom.

4. After identifying the idiom correctly, your partner chooses a card from his or her pile and gives a definition or sentence.

5. Continue back and forth until you and your partner have correctly guessed all the idioms.

B. Round-Robin Story

Complete the following story in small groups.

1. One student adds to the story that begins below, using one of the idioms from this chapter.

2. The next student continues the story, using another idiom from this chapter.

3. Continue until all the idioms have been used and the story has ended.

> One night I had a very strange dream. I was walking down the street when, out of the blue, . . .

C. Role Play

Perform a role play in pairs.

1. Imagine that you are one of the characters at the top of page 86. You may refer to the script of *The Bermuda Triangle* on page 76 for background information.

2. Write a script for a role play. Use as many of the idioms from this chapter as you can.

3. Practice the role play.

4. Perform the role play for your classmates.

RANDY: You just came back from a cruise to Bermuda. One night, you and your friends were walking around on the ship. Suddenly, you felt a strange force pulling you toward the water. At the same time, you noticed flashing lights in the sky. Your friends were afraid and went inside, but you stayed outside. After a few minutes, everything seemed fine. Tell the reporter about your experience.

REPORTER: You don't really believe Randy's story. You think Randy had too much to drink or has a good imagination. However, you are writing a newspaper report about the Bermuda Triangle, so you need information. Ask Randy questions to find out the truth.

USING THE IDIOMS IN WRITING

D. Writing with Idioms

Imagine that you live in the year 1500. You are an explorer who travels to faraway places that people from your country have never visited.

Write a letter to your family or friends at home. Tell them about your adventures. Be sure to answer the following questions.

- Where have you traveled?

- Who have you met?

- What have you found?

Use at least four of the idioms from this chapter.

E. Advertising with Idioms

Create an ad for a product or service.

1. Choose a product or service that you would like to advertise.

2. Determine your audience—the people most likely to buy your product or service.

3. Write a slogan for your ad, using one or more of the idioms from this chapter.

4. Decide on what picture(s) you will use in your ad.

5. Write the rest of your ad.

6. Present your ad to the class. Do your classmates understand your use of the idiom? Would they buy your product or service?

REVIEW II

Chapters 4–6

I. Questions and Answers

Work in pairs. Ask each other questions and answer them. Student A's questions and answers are below. Student B's questions and answers are on page 88. Do not show each other your questions and answers.

STUDENT A

Part A

Ask the questions below. Student B will answer. Check the answers.

1. Have you already wrapped six presents?
2. Did you believe that Kathy could play the trumpet?
3. Are you and your friends going to the movies tonight?
4. Are you going to take flying lessons?
5. Did you expect to see your brother here?

Part B

Student B will ask questions. Choose the best answer from the list below. Student B will check the answers.

a. Yes, my friends made fun of me.
b. No, I've got to hand it to her.
c. No, he pulled the wool over my eyes.
d. Yes! Then I would be on Easy Street.
e. No, they paid the price.
f. No. Now I'm in a real jam.
g. Yes. So far, I've stayed on track.

STUDENT B

Part A

Student A will ask questions. Choose the best answer from the list below. Student A will check the answers.

a. Yes, I'm on a roll now.

b. No, I beg to differ with her.

c. No, I didn't take her seriously until I heard her play.

d. No, his visit came out of the blue.

e. Yes, although my mother thinks I'm playing with fire.

f. Yes, I saw right through her.

g. I'm not sure. It's up to them to decide what to do.

Part B

Ask the questions below. Student A will answer. Check the answers.

1. Would you like to win the lottery?

2. Are you still on your diet?

3. Did you know that Joe was lying?

4. Did you find someone to work for you on Friday night?

5. Did anyone say anything about your new haircut?

II. Idiom Puzzler

Solve the following crossword puzzle. The clues are on page 90.

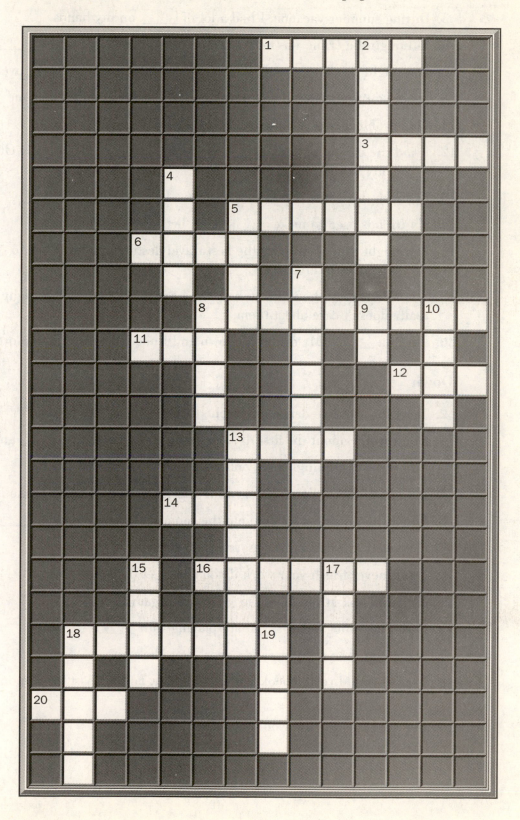

Across

1. My grandfather smoked too much, and now he's paying the _____ .

3. During summer vacation, I had a lot of _____ on my hands.

5. Although the crime was hard to solve, the detective got to the _____ of it.

6. You might think you can trick me, but you can't pull the _____ over my eyes!

8. I said you would lose if you didn't practice, but you didn't take me _____ .

11. This problem is very difficult to understand. I don't _____ it.

12. I said the capital of Canada is Toronto. When I learned it's really Ottawa, I had to _____ my words.

13. I've won this game three times in a row. I'm on a _____ .

14. My friends used to make _____ of me because I had big ears.

16. You might think Europe is the best travel destination, but I beg to _____ . I think Africa is more interesting.

18. The senator says he wants to help the homeless, but I can see right _____ him. He really doesn't care about them.

20. I'm in a _____ . My car broke down and I need to get to the airport immediately.

Down

2. Terry loves to live dangerously. She throws _____ to the wind.

4. Don't worry about the first day of school. Just go with the _____ and you'll be OK.

5. The sun was shining. Then, out of the _____ , it started to rain.

7. If your mother tells you to eat your vegetables, you shouldn't take it _____ .

8. When the president walked into the room, he created quite a _____ .

9. How well you do in this class is _____ to you.

10. You'll never finish your work if you don't get the _____ out.

13. Oh, no! Look at the time! I'm _____ late again.

15. If you take illegal drugs, you are playing with _____ .

17. Madeleine won the lottery last year. Now she's on _____ Street.

18. I said I would read a book a week this year. For the past three months, I've stayed on _____.

19. I've got to _____ it to you. Your report was excellent.

ADVICE

How To Be A Smart Cookie.

'Tis the season to bake cookies. Read on to find out ways to make yours as good as they can be. Like using the one flour more smart cookie bakers use than any other. Gold Medal Flour.

Start with the best ingredients for cookie dough that's smooth, easy to roll, and won't tear or crumble. Gold Medal must pass 15 strict quality checks so you can be sure it's the best it can be.

Be careful not to overwork your dough. Avoid rolling more than twice. The result could be tough cookies. Refrigerating your dough before rolling will also make your cookies more tender.

We continually bake cookies under home conditions in the Betty Crocker Kitchens. It helps us guarantee that the cookies you bake will be your best time after time, batch after batch.

© 1993 General Mills, Inc.

Gold MEDAL

AMERICA'S #1 FLOUR

ALL-PURPOSE

ENRICHED • BLEACHED • PRESIFTED FLOUR

Bake with Gold Medal.® America's #1 flour.

Reprinted with permission of General Mills.

I Learning the Idioms

WARMING UP

Complete the following activities in pairs or small groups. Compare answers and discuss with your classmates.

1. What should you do in the following situations? Discuss solutions to these problems.

   • Your friend is engaged and very excited about getting married. However, you know that her fiancé is still seeing his old girlfriend.

   • Your friend told you he was going away for the weekend and would be back on Sunday night. However, it is now Tuesday, and he hasn't returned.

   • Your friend is trying to find a good job. She buys a new outfit and gets her hair cut. You think she looks terrible. What should you do?

2. Write at least two pieces of advice for someone who:

   • is going to have a baby.

   • is going to visit you in your country.

   • is looking for a new job.

   • always fights with a teenage son or daughter.

   • has been accepted to a good university.

   • has just stopped dating a boyfriend or girlfriend.

   • is taking his or her first airplane ride.

   • has to cook dinner for his or her boss.

   • is going to meet the president of your country.

3. Write down a problem that you have. Ask your classmates for advice.

GETTING TO KNOW THE IDIOMS

A. Listening for Understanding

Listen to the radio show What Should I Do? *Think about the following questions. Then discuss your answers in pairs or small groups.*

1. What is Caller 1's problem? What advice do Bob and Paula give her? Do you agree? Why or why not?

2. What is Caller 2's problem? What advice do Bob and Paula give him? Do you agree? Why or why not?

3. What is Caller 3's problem? Have you ever been to a party where you didn't know anyone? What did you do?

4. Do Bob and Paula always agree with each other? Do you always agree with their advice? Explain.

B. Identifying the Idioms

The idioms listed below are used throughout the radio show you just heard. Read the script of the radio show on pages 94–95. Underline the idioms. Number them on the list below in the order they occur. Try to guess the meaning of each idiom by looking at how it is used.

____ chicken   ____ right up one's alley

____ get over something   ____ smart cookie

____ go against the grain   ____ way to go

____ make no bones about it   ____ word of mouth

What Should I Do?

HOST: It's time for the radio show *What Should I Do?*, in which members of our audience call in for advice. Today, we're giving advice about friends who have problems. If you have a friend with a problem, just call in and ask, "What should I do?" Bob and Paula, our advice experts, will help you solve it.

PAULA: Caller Number 1, you're on the air. What can we do for you?

CALLER 1: Hi, Bob and Paula! My best friend just told me that she's getting married. She'd like me to be the maid of honor at her wedding. The problem is that she's marrying *my* old boyfriend, and I don't want to see him! What should I do?

BOB: Oh, get over it! If they're happy together, then you should be happy, too. Hide your true feelings and say *yes*!

PAULA: Bob, I agree! Tell your friend, "Way to go!" You should be excited to be her maid of honor. Forget about your relationship with your old boyfriend—he's going to be *her* husband now.

BOB: Paula, why don't we take the next caller. Caller Number 2, are you there?

CALLER 2: Yes, hi. My name's Eric. I'm worried about my friend. He wants to join a club that seems strange to me. The leader of the club makes the members live together. They have to give him all their money. He won't even let them talk to their old friends. What should I do?

PAULA: Eric, I think you're a smart cookie to recognize that something is wrong. First, you should find out everything you can about this club. Talk to former members. Talk to current members. Word of mouth is the best way to get information. Then talk to your friend.

BOB: Make no bones about it, your friend is *certainly* making a big mistake. The leader of the club is trying to control the members. He'll probably punish anyone who goes against the grain. Try to convince your friend not to join!

PAULA: Now on to Caller Number 3. What's your question?

CALLER 3:   My friend was invited to a party and he asked me to go with him. I agreed, but today he told me that he can't go. Should I go to the party without him? I won't know anyone there!

PAULA: Sure! A party is a party, so go and have fun. You may make some new friends! Maybe you'll even meet someone with interests that are right up your alley—just the things that *you're* interested in.

BOB: I don't think it's that easy, Paula. I'm chicken about going to parties by myself. I think meeting strangers and talking to them is a lot of work. However, you might meet some interesting people, so if you feel brave, do it! And good luck.

HOST: Thanks for being with us today on *What Should I Do?* Join us tomorrow for another session with Bob and Paula!

C. Getting the Meaning

Look at the underlined phrase in each of the following statements. Pay attention to how the idiom is used, and try to guess its meaning. You may also refer to the script of What Should I Do? *on pages 94–95. Choose from the definitions below. Write the letter on the line.*

___f___   1. "I won first place in the horse show!" "<u>Way to go</u>!"

_____   2. Before newspapers were invented, news was spread by <u>word of mouth</u>.

_____   3. I can't <u>get over</u> the fact that my youngest son is getting married!

_____   4. Mona graduated from college when she was only twenty. She's a s<u>mart cookie</u>.

_____   5. Richard <u>makes no bones about</u> his support for capital punishment.

_____   6. That art museum was <u>right up my alley</u>. I loved it!

_____   7. I'm too <u>chicken</u> to go on the big roller coaster.

_____   8. Most people in this town are Republicans. If you vote Democrat, you're <u>going against the grain</u>.

a. to accept a difficult or surprising situation

b. perfectly matched to one's interests

c. by one person speaking to another

d. to behave differently than others

e. afraid or nervous

f. congratulations

g. a very clever person

h. to have no doubt about something

PRACTICING THE IDIOMS

D. Choosing the Best Answer

Listen to each short conversation that takes place at a party and to the questions that follow. Read the sentences below. Choose the sentence that best answers each question you heard. Circle a or b.

Conversation A

1. a. It was in the newspaper.
   b. People talked about it. *(circled)*

2. a. They've accepted it.
   b. They haven't accepted it.

3. a. No, she doesn't.
   b. Yes, she does.

Conversation B

1. a. She wanted to ask him for a favor.
   b. She wanted to congratulate him.

2. a. He was nervous.
   b. He was happy.

Conversation C

1. a. Because she is interested in doing the project.
   b. Because the project matches her interests.

2. a. She's sure she couldn't do it.
   b. It's no secret she'd enjoy it.

3. a. He's very clever.
   b. His job is easier than Julie's.

E. Retelling the Story

Read the script of What Should I Do? *on pages 94–95 again. The sentences below refer to statements in that script. Restate the sentences, using the appropriate idioms. Try to write them <u>without</u> looking at the script again.*

1. Bob said the first caller should accept the fact that her friend and former boyfriend are getting married.

   Bob told the first caller to get over the fact that her ex-boyfriend is

   marrying her friend.

2. Paula said that she should congratulate her friend.

   _____

3. Paula said the second caller was very clever to notice a problem with his friend's club.

   _____

4. Paula said the best way to get information is to talk to other people.

   _____

5. Bob said he was certain that Eric's friend was making a mistake.

   _____

6. Bob thought the club leader would punish members who act differently than others.

   _____

7. Paula told the third caller she might meet people with similar interests at the party.

   _____

8. Bob said he is nervous about going to parties by himself.

   _____

F. Putting the Idioms Into Practice

Imagine that your friends have the following problems. Read the problems carefully. Give your friends advice, using the idioms in parentheses. Change the form of the idioms as needed to fit your answer.

1. I love to play the piano. My school is looking for someone to play the piano for the choir. Should I do it? (right up one's alley)

   _Sure! It sounds like that's right up your alley._____

2. I have very good grades in school. My parents want me to go to college. However, I'm worried that I won't be accepted. What should I do? (smart cookie)

   _____

3. My friend and I entered the same contest. I didn't win anything, but he got first place. I'm jealous. What should I do? (Way to go!)

   _____

4. I hadn't seen my ex-girlfriend for seven months. Last week, I saw her with another man. I was angry. What should I do? (get over something)

   _____

5. When I go out with my friends, they like to go to different international restaurants and try new foods. I'm afraid to eat strange foods. What should I do? (chicken)

   _____

6. Some of my friends have started to take illegal drugs. I think that's a bad idea. What should I do? (make no bones about it)

   _____

7. Many of my friends think it's OK to cheat on school assignments. I don't cheat, and my grades are not as good as theirs. What should I do? (go against the grain)

   _____

8. Yesterday I heard something terrible about one of my friends. I don't think it's true, but I'm not sure. What should I do? (word of mouth)

   _____

II Finding the Idioms in Ads

INTERPRETING THE ADS

Look at the following ads. Determine what is being advertised. Find the featured idiom in each ad and review its meaning. Then answer the questions.

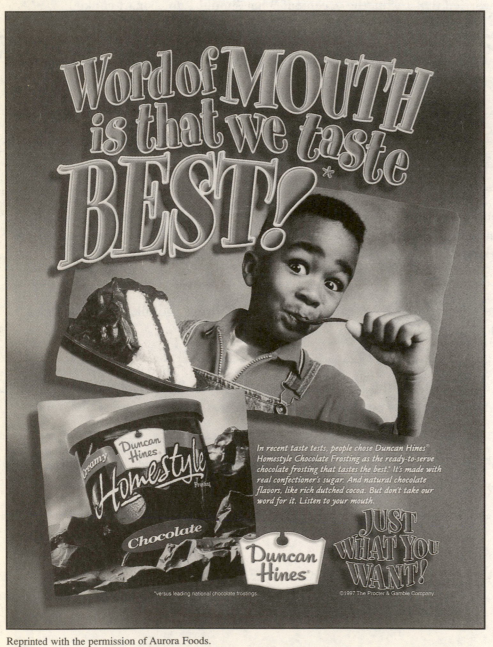

Reprinted with the permission of Aurora Foods.

1. Describe the picture. Where is the boy's spoon?

2. According to this ad, most people who tried this frosting said it tastes better than other frostings. How does this relate to the idiom in the ad?

3. Is the phrase *word of mouth* used idiomatically, literally, or both ways? Explain.

Reprinted with permission of General Mills.

1. What product is being advertised?

2. How can Gold Medal flour make you a *smart cookie*?

1. What product is being advertised? What does it do?

2. What is being cooked?

3. Explain the slogan *Better than restaurant rotisserie. (And we're not too chicken to say so.)*.

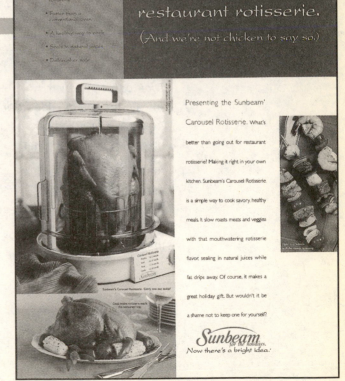

Reprinted with the permission of Sunbeam Corporation.

1. What is this product? What does it do?

2. How has the idiom been changed in this ad? Why do you think it was changed?

3. Explain how the idiom *make no bones about it* relates to the product.

1. Who are Tom and Dick? Who is Harry?

2. What is Invisible Fencing? What is its purpose?

3. In the sentence *Tom & Dick can't get over Invisible Fencing*, does *get over* have an idiomatic or literal meaning? Explain.

4. In the sentence *Neither can Harry (get over Invisible Fencing)*, does *get over* have an idiomatic or literal meaning? Explain.

1. The word *grain* refers to wood fibers. What is pictured in the ad? Can you see the grain?

2. The advertiser is Louisiana-Pacific. What do you think it produces?

3. According to this ad, about twenty years ago people became concerned about cutting down old trees because doing so harms the environment. This company now uses small pieces of wood from fast-growing trees to make its products. How did this company *go against the grain*? How did it *change the grain*?

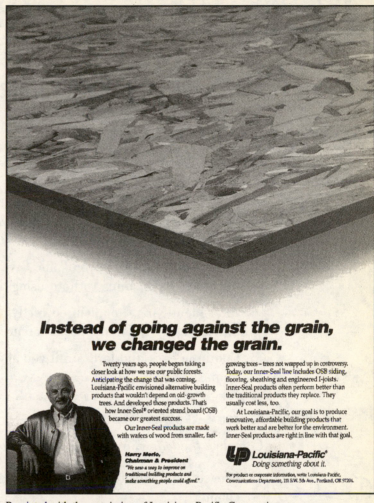

Instead of going against the grain, we changed the grain.

Twenty years ago, people began taking a closer look at how we use our public forests. Anticipating the change that was coming, Louisiana-Pacific envisioned alternative building products that wouldn't depend on old-growth trees. And developed those products. That's how Inner-Seal® oriented strand board (OSB) became our greatest success.

Our Inner-Seal products are made with wafers of wood from smaller, fast-growing trees – trees not wrapped up in controversy. Today, our Inner-Seal line includes OSB siding, flooring, sheathing and engineered I-joists. Inner-Seal products often perform better than the traditional products they replace. They usually cost less, too.

At Louisiana-Pacific, our goal is to produce innovative, affordable building products that work better and are better for the environment. Inner-Seal products are right in line with that goal.

Harry Merlo, Chairman & President
"We saw a way to improve on traditional building products and make something people could afford."

⊔ℙ Louisiana-Pacific®
Doing something about it.

For product or corporate information, write Louisiana-Pacific, Communications Department, 111 S.W. 5th Ave., Portland, OR 97204.

Reprinted with the permission of Louisiana-Pacific Corporation.

THINKING ABOUT THE ADS

Review the ads in this chapter. Choose the one that you like best. Complete the following statements based on that ad.

1. The ad that I like the best is . . . because . . . .

2. I think Americans would like this ad because . . . .

3. It is important to many Americans to . . . .

4. Other examples in American life that show how Americans feel about this value are . . . .

5. People from my country would/would not like this ad because . . . .

III Using the Idioms

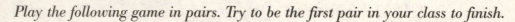

USING THE IDIOMS IN SPEECH

A. Name That Idiom!

Play the following game in pairs. Try to be the first pair in your class to finish.

1. With a partner, copy the idioms from the list on page 91 onto separate index cards.

2. Divide the cards into two piles. Give one pile to your partner. Do not look at each other's cards.

3. Choose one card from your pile. Give a definition of the idiom or a sentence that illustrates its meaning <u>without</u> using the idiom.

4. After identifying the idiom correctly, your partner chooses a card from his or her pile and gives a definition or sentence.

5. Continue back and forth until you and your partner have correctly guessed all the idioms.

B. Round-Robin Story

Complete the following story in small groups.

1. One student adds to the story that begins below, using one of the idioms from this chapter.

2. The next student continues the story, using another idiom from this chapter.

3. Continue until all the idioms have been used and the story has ended.

    Maya was a very intelligent woman with many talents and hobbies. But there was one thing she couldn't do. She was afraid of speaking in public. Once, when she was invited to give a speech, she prepared for weeks. However, when she stood up in front of the audience, she forgot everything and had to sit back down. It was embarrassing, but she was too chicken to stand up again. Maya didn't know what to do. Then, one day she saw a billboard with the message: ARE YOU AFRAID OF SOMETHING? PROFESSOR SIMON CAN HELP YOU! . . .

C. Role Play

Perform a role play in small groups.

1. Imagine that you are one of the characters in the situation described below. You may refer to the script of *What Should I Do?* on page 94–95 for background information.

2. Write a script for a role play. Use as many of the idioms from this chapter as you can.

3. Practice the role play.

4. Perform the role play for your classmates.

CALLER: A friend told you that he stole thousands of dollars. He asked you to promise not to tell anyone about the crime. However, now your friend has disappeared. You think his disappearance is related to the stolen money. Call the radio show *What Should I Do?* and ask Bob and Paula for advice.

BOB: You think a promise is a promise. It's important to be loyal to your friends, even if others expect you to act differently. Advise the caller to continue to keep this secret.

PAULA: You think the caller should tell the police the whole story. It's necessary to find the friend and make sure he is safe. Advise the caller to go to the police immediately.

USING THE IDIOMS IN WRITING

D. Writing with Idioms

Imagine that you write a newspaper advice column.

Recently, you received the following letter from one of your readers. Respond to the letter, giving advice for the problem. Be sure to use at least four idioms from this chapter in your letter.

> Dear _____ ,
> <small>your name</small>
>
> I have been working at my job for many years, and I'm a very good worker. Recently my boss hired someone else to help in the office. She doesn't do her job well, but she's very pretty. My boss started giving her more work than he gives me, and he pays more attention to her. At first I was glad to have some help, but now I'm not happy at all. I'm afraid to talk to my boss about this, because I know he likes her a lot. Also, someone told me that they're dating. This is a good job and I don't want to lose it. What should I do?
>
> Worried at Work

E.   Advertising with Idioms

Create an ad for a product or service.

1. Choose a product or service that you would like to advertise.

2. Determine your audience—the people most likely to buy your product or service.

3. Write a slogan for your ad, using one or more of the idioms from this chapter.

4. Decide what picture(s) you will use in your ad.

5. Write the rest of your ad.

6. Present your ad to the class. Do your classmates understand your use of the idiom? Would they buy your product or service?

Chapter 8

LAST WISHES

Idioms

CATCH ON

CUT THE MUSTARD

EARN ONE'S STRIPES

GET CARRIED AWAY

ONE'S SHIP HAS COME IN

OUT OF THE QUESTION

UPPER CRUST

WINDOW-SHOPPING

"*H*ow to buy a casket without getting carried away."

– *Arnold Saltsman, General Manager*

Casket prices everywhere have gotten out of hand, forcing many families to consider alternatives. In response, we've taken the initiative to lower our casket prices...so you won't have to lower your

MOUNT SINAI
MEMORIAL PARKS
and MORTUARY

A Friend of the Family™

Dedicated to the entire Jewish Community as a service of Sinai Temple of Los Angeles.   LOS ANGELES • SIMI VALLEY (800) 600-0076

I Learning the Idioms

WARMING UP

Complete the following activities in pairs or small groups. Compare answers and discuss with your classmates.

1. A *will* is a legal document that describes how a person wants personal property to be distributed after his or her death. Imagine that you are preparing to write your will.

   - Make a list of three items that you own (besides money). You want to give each item to a different person in your class.
   - Discuss the items. To whom would you give each item?
   - Write a will, following the format below.

     I leave ___my English books___ to ___Marie___ .

     because ___she loves to study English___ .

2. Imagine that you have a rich uncle who just died. He left you a choice of one of the following three items in his will. However, certain conditions apply to each item. Which item would you choose? Explain your reasons.

   - A beautiful house valued at $750,000. However, you may not sell it until you have lived in it for at least five years, and it is in a different city. You do not want to live in that city.
   - Stock in a company worth $250,000. However, you may not sell the stock for at least five years. The value of the stock has varied a lot lately. In five years, it may be worth a lot more than $250,000 or worth almost nothing.
   - $100,000. However, you must spend it all within one month.

GETTING TO KNOW THE IDIOMS

A. Listening for Understanding

*Listen to the story about the McDonald family. Think about the following questions.
Then discuss your answers in pairs or small groups.*

1. What was Quincy McDonald's life like when he was a child? How is it different
   now?

2. What kind of life have Mr. McDonald's children had?

3. Describe Henry. What do you think he is like? What do you think his father
   should leave him? Why?

4. Describe Tiffany's life. What should her father leave her? Why?

5. Describe Sterling. What should Mr. McDonald leave him? Why?

B. Identifying the Idioms

*The idioms listed below are used throughout the story you just heard. Read the script of
the story on page 110. Underline the idioms. Number them on the list below in the order
they occur. Try to guess the meaning of each idiom by looking at how it is used.*

____ catch on   ____ one's ship has come in

____ cut the mustard   ____ out of the question

____ earn one's stripes   ____ upper crust

____ get carried away   ____ window-shopping

Last Wishes

Quincy McDonald is writing his will. He has three children, and he wants each of them to receive the proper inheritance. Mr. McDonald is very rich, but when he was young his family was quite poor. He earned his stripes selling newspapers on the street corner, and he eventually became the president and owner of a large company. Mr. McDonald knows what it's like to be poor. However, his children were born into the upper crust and have had an easy life. He has divided his property into three parts: his money, his house, and his art collection. How should Mr. McDonald distribute his property?

Henry, the oldest, loves to gamble, so giving him money is out of the question. He might get carried away and spend it all on gambling. However, he is a very good businessman and has done well in his father's company.

Tiffany, the middle child, lives in a large mansion with many servants. Her ship came in when she married her husband, who is even richer than Mr. McDonald. She loves to spend her days window-shopping. Tiffany is very intelligent and often helps her husband with his investments.

Sterling, the youngest child, is a hard worker, but he's not very smart. He was admitted to a college, but he couldn't cut the mustard. His grades were so bad that he had to leave. He tried working for his father, but he never caught on to the business, so he quit. Mr. McDonald knows that Sterling will need a lot of help to be successful, even though he works harder than his brother or sister.

Which one of Mr. McDonald's children should receive the money? Who should get the house? Who should inherit the art collection? Why? What can Mr. McDonald do to make sure that his children take care of their inheritance?

C. Getting the Meaning

Look at the underlined phrase in each of the following statements. Pay attention to how the idiom is used, and try to guess its meaning. You may also refer to the script of Last Wishes *on page 110. Choose from the definitions below. Write the letter on the line.*

  <u>e</u>   1 You can't afford a room at that hotel; it's only for the <u>upper crust</u>.

  _____   2. I love to go <u>window-shopping</u> at expensive stores, although I would never buy
              anything there.

  _____   3. I was only going to write a short note to my grandparents, but I <u>got carried away</u> and wrote a ten-page letter.

  _____   4. Although Martin never learned to drive as a teenager, I think he will <u>catch on</u> quickly.

  _____   5. You'll have to rewrite this report. Without major changes, it will never <u>cut the mustard</u>.

  _____   6. When <u>my ship comes in</u>, I'm going to buy a vacation home in Europe.

  _____   7. Carl <u>earned his stripes</u> working at every job in the advertising company. Now he's the president and everyone respects him.

  _____   8. You may not stay out until midnight. It's <u>out of the question</u>.

a. to be good enough

b. someone has become rich

c. to lose one's self-control and do too much of something

d. to earn respect through hard work and success

e. the richest or highest class of society

f. impossible

g. looking at items in stores without buying them

h. to learn; to understand

PRACTICING THE IDIOMS

D. Choosing the Best Answer

Listen to each short conversation and to the statement that follows. Circle T *if the statement is true and* F *if it is false.*

1. (T) / F   2. T / F   3. T / F   4. T / F

5. T / F   6. T / F   7. T / F   8. T / F

E.   Retelling the Story

Read the script of Last Wishes *on page 110 again. The sentences below refer to sentences in that script. Restate the sentences, using the appropriate idioms. Try to write them **without** looking at the story again.*

1. Quincy McDonald worked hard and earned respect by selling newspapers on a street corner.

   <u>Quincy McDonald earned his stripes by selling newspapers on a street corner.</u>

2. Mr. McDonald's children were born into the richest class of society.

   _____

3. It is impossible for Mr. McDonald to leave his money to Henry.

   _____

4. Henry might lose control and spend all the money on gambling.

   _____

5. Tiffany got the wealth she'd hoped for when she married her husband.

   _____

6. Tiffany loves to spend her time looking for things to buy.

   _____

7. Sterling started college, but he wasn't smart enough to finish.

   _____

8. Sterling tried to work in his father's business, but he didn't understand it.

   _____

F.   Putting the Idioms into Practice

Read the newspaper column on page 113. It contains gossip, or rumors, about famous people. Complete the sentences with appropriate idioms from the list.

carried away	his ship has come in
catch on	out of the question
cut the mustard	upper crust
earned his stripes	window-shopping

Once again it is time to look at the week in review here at *Star Gossip*, where we always tell you the most important news about your favorite stars and celebrities.

Famous movie director Frank Spellman said he will never allow actress Mimi Monroe to appear in another one of his movies. "It's ____out of the question____,"
1.
he told reporters. "Her acting skills are terrible! None of her scenes

_____ in my last movie." We would suggest that Mimi take
2.
some acting classes, or her career in Hollywood may be over.

In other news, the rock star Laddie Baddie has died of a drug overdose. His death comes only one month after *Roll and Rock* magazine said, "Everybody is buying Laddie Baddie's records! Finally, _____. After years of playing
3.
in small clubs all over the country, he has _____. He is certain
4.
to be one of the most successful rock stars of the year." Mr. Baddie's agent said, "This is a very sad time, but I hope that his death will help other young music stars

_____ to the danger of using drugs."
5.

Finally, we have big news about TV star Tim Rivers, who has broken more hearts than we can count. We heard that he and his current girlfriend, Rita Masters, are _____ for a diamond ring! Rita comes from the
6.
_____ of New York City society. We heard reports that she
7.
got _____ when she met Tim, and was making wedding plans
8.
the same day. Of course, we know that she certainly isn't his first girlfriend, so we'll let you know what happens.

II Finding the Idioms in Ads

INTERPRETING THE ADS

Look at the following ads. Determine what is being advertised. Find the featured idiom in each ad and review its meaning. Then answer the questions.

1. Describe the picture.

2. What does *indulgent* mean? Who is being indulgent in the ad? Why?

3. Explain the sentence *Now you're catching on.*

1. What is a *casket*? How is this connected to the literal meaning of *get carried away*?

2. Explain the idiomatic meaning of the slogan *How to buy a casket without getting carried away.*

3. The idiom *out of hand* means "out of control." Explain the sentence *Casket prices everywhere have gotten out of hand, forcing many families to consider alternatives.*

"*How* to buy a casket without getting carried away."
— *Arnold Saltzman, General Manager*

Casket prices everywhere have gotten out of hand, forcing many families to consider alternatives. In response, we've taken the initiative to lower our casket prices...so you won't have to lower your

Dedicated to the entire Jewish Community as a service of Sinai Temple of Los Angeles.

MOUNT SINAI MEMORIAL PARKS and MORTUARY
A Friend of the Family™
LOS ANGELES • SIMI VALLEY (800) 600-0076

Reprinted with the permission of Mount Sinai Memorial Parks and Mortuary, Los Angeles.

AAA members. Your ship has come in.

7-DAY ITINERARY
S.S.INDEPENDENCE
Saturday Honolulu, Oahu
Sunday At Sea
Monday Nawiliwili, Kauai
Tuesday Kahului, Maui
Wednesday Kahului, Maui
Thursday Hilo, Hawaii
Friday Kona, Hawaii
Saturday Honolulu, Oahu

To all of you who have been dreaming of a cruise through paradise, we would like to offer this delightful dose of reality. Your ship has just come in. We're American Hawaii Cruises, and we're offering you a special discount rate when you book through your AAA travel agent. In 7 days we'll take you, round trip, from Honolulu as we explore Kauai, Maui, and the Big Island. You'll see more of Hawaii than you ever dreamed existed. And because you're a member of AAA, you can receive two additional free nights in a Waikiki hotel. Call you AAA travel agent now for more information.

AMERICAN HAWAII CRUISES®

Reprinted with the permission of American Hawaii Cruises.

1. AAA, or the American Automobile Association, is an organization that provides help if your car stops working. It also provides reduced prices for some types of vacations. What kind of vacation is this ad for?

2. Explain the literal meaning of *Your ship has come in.*

3. Explain the idiomatic meaning of *Your ship has come in.*

Reprinted with the permission of Samsonite.

1. What product is being advertised?

2. Who is the intended audience for the product?

3. What animal is pictured? How does it relate to the slogan *Reserved for those who have earned their stripes*?

Reprinted with the permission of Reckitt & Coleman Inc.

1. Describe the picture. What spilled on the carpet?

2. What did Resolve do? How did it *cut the mustard*?

3. What is the message of this ad?

1. A *pot pie* is a pie made with meat and vegetables. Most pies have a bottom *crust*, or pastry layer, and some also have a top crust. Explain the slogan *A Bisquick pot pie is strictly upper crust.*

2. What kind of image are the advertisers trying to give this pot pie?

3. Who do you think will buy this product? Why?

With the permission of General Mills, Inc.

THINKING ABOUT THE ADS

Review the ads in this chapter. Choose the one that you like best. Complete the following statements based on that ad.

1. The ad that I like the best is . . . because . . . .

2. I think Americans would like this ad because . . . .

3. It is important to many Americans to . . . .

4. Other examples in American life that show how Americans feel about this value are . . . .

5. People from my country would/would not like this ad because . . . .

III Using the Idioms

USING THE IDIOMS IN SPEECH

A. Name That Idiom!

Play the following game in pairs. Try to be the first pair in your class to finish.

1. With a partner, copy the idioms from the list on page 107 onto separate index cards.

2. Divide the cards into two piles. Give one pile to your partner. Do not look at each other's cards.

3. Choose one card from your pile. Give a definition of the idiom or a sentence that illustrates its meaning <u>without</u> using the idiom.

4. After identifying the idiom correctly, your partner chooses a card from his or her pile and gives a definition or sentence.

5. Continue back and forth until you and your partner have correctly guessed all the idioms.

B. Round-Robin Story

Complete the following story in small groups.

1. One student adds to the story that begins below, using one of the idioms from this chapter.

2. The next student continues the story, using another idiom from this chapter.

3. Continue until all the idioms have been used and the story has ended.

    Jake had bad luck. For two years, he'd been homeless, and his clothes were torn and dirty. But every day he found work, and at the end of the day he bought some food for his dinner and a lottery ticket. Jake knew that someday his ship would come in . . . .

C. Role Play

Perform a role play in pairs.

1. Imagine that you are one of the characters at the top of page 119. You may refer to the script of *Last Wishes* on page 110 for background information.

2. Write a script for a role play. Use as many of the idioms from this chapter as you can.

3. Practice the role play.

4. Perform the role play for your classmates.

MR. MCDONALD: You love all your children very much, and you want them to be happy. Tell your son/daughter how you've decided to divide your property after you die. Explain why.

SON/DAUGHTER: You were hoping to get something different after your father's death. Try to convince him to change his will.

USING THE IDIOMS IN WRITING

D. Writing with Idioms

Imagine that you are the valedictorian at a university.

1. Write a graduation speech. Tell your classmates how to be successful in today's world. Include some of the following suggestions.

   • Learn as much as you can. You will quickly understand what you have to do.
   • Work hard. A lazy person will never be successful.
   • It takes a long time to earn people's respect.
   • If you don't give up, you'll reach the highest level of society.
   • If you become rich, don't get so excited that you spend all your money.

   Use at least four idioms from this chapter.

2. Be prepared to give the speech in class.

E. Advertising with Idioms

Create an ad for a product or service.

1. Choose a product or service that you would like to advertise.

2. Determine your audience—the people most likely to buy your product or service.

3. Write a slogan for your ad, using one or more of the idioms from this chapter.

4. Decide on what picture(s) you will use in your ad.

5. Write the rest of your ad.

6. Present your ad to the class. Do your classmates understand your use of the idiom? Would they buy your product or service?

Chapter 9

PREDICTIONS

Idioms

IN ONE'S BLOOD

LOOK FORWARD TO SOMETHING

MEASURE UP

NOTHING TO SNEEZE AT

ON THE OTHER HAND

PUT SOMETHING ON HOLD

RUN IN THE FAMILY

SHORT ON SOMETHING

Printed with the permission of Mars, Incorporated.

I Learning the Idioms

WARMING UP

Complete the following activities in pairs or small groups. Compare answers and discuss with your classmates.

1. Discuss the following questions.

   • Do you think it is possible to predict the future? Why or why not?

   • Have you ever gone to a fortune-teller? If so, describe the experience.

   • Would you like to know exactly what will happen in the future? Why or why not?

2. Imagine that you are a fortune-teller. Your partner wants to know what will happen in the future. Make predictions about the following areas of your partner's life:

   love   family   career
   money   travel   health

   Then have your partner make predictions about your future.

3. Discuss your partner's predictions about your future. Which do you think will happen? Which do you think will not happen? Explain.

4. On your own, write a paragraph describing your life ten years from now. Use your partner's predictions and your own ideas. Share your paragraph with the class.

GETTING TO KNOW THE IDIOMS

A. Listening for Understanding

Listen to the story about a fortune-teller's predictions. Think about the following questions. Then discuss your answers in pairs or small groups.

1. How much does the fortune-teller usually charge? How much did she charge the customer?

2. How much does the fortune-teller want to charge the customer the next time? Why?

3. Does the fortune-teller focus on the customer's love life, career, or family?

4. What does she predict will happen to the customer?

5. According to the fortune-teller, how will the customer become rich?

6. Do you think the fortune-teller and the customer will meet again? Why or why not?

B. Identifying the Idioms

The idioms listed below are used throughout the story you just heard. Read the script of the recording on page 123. Underline the idioms. Number them on the list below in the order they occur. Try to guess the meaning of each idiom by looking at how it is used.

____ in one's blood   ____ on the other hand

____ look forward to something ____ put something on hold

____ measure up   ____ run in the family

____ nothing to sneeze at   ____ short on something

The Fortune-Teller

The fortune-teller peeked out from behind a dark curtain and smiled at me. The sign in front of her tent was bright with flashing lights. It read: SEE YOUR FUTURE! ONLY $20! She pushed the curtain back and said in a low voice, "Come in! Come in! Don't be afraid. I can see everything!" I was very curious.

"I'm sorry," I said. "I'm a little short on cash. Maybe another time."

"Aaaah," she whispered, "there is no better time than now. For you, this once, it is only $10. But the next time you visit me, you'll have so much money, you will give me $50!"

"Really?" I said, handing her a $10 bill. "Then I can look forward to being rich?"

"Well . . . perhaps." She sat in a large chair and closed her eyes. "It depends on how hard you are willing to work. Especially after you lose your job."

"What?" I said angrily. "This is terrible news. How will I ever get rich if I lose my job?"

"Don't worry so much," replied the fortune-teller. "It seems like bad news, but on the other hand, it may be very good. The work you do now does not measure up. Isn't that right?" She was right, and I nodded my head. "I can see that you want to do something different. You are very creative. You are an artist, right? I can tell that it's in your blood."

"Well," I said, "my mother is an artist, and so was my grandfather. So I guess it runs in my family. And I also love to draw and paint."

"Good, good," said the fortune-teller, smiling as if she had a secret. "But it will not be easy at first. Still, you mustn't get discouraged. You'll have to put many things in your life on hold. You'll have to wait to get the things you want. It may be a long time. But then . . . ." She stopped speaking and closed her eyes again.

"What? What will happen then?" I shouted.

"Then," she opened her eyes wide, "then something will happen. Something good. You will have a wonderful opportunity."

"What is it?" I asked.

"I don't know, but it will certainly be nothing to sneeze at. You may become famous. And after that, you will never be short on money again."

The fortune-teller rose from her chair and opened the curtain. "That's all for now. But remember," she said as I got up to leave, "next time it is $50!"

"If what you say is true," I said as I left, "then I will gladly look forward to our next meeting."

It was probably a silly waste of money. But on the other hand, what if she really was a fortune-teller with mysterious powers?

C. Getting the Meaning

Look at the underlined phrase in each of the following statements. Pay attention to how the idiom is used, and try to guess its meaning. You may also refer to the script of The Fortune-Teller *on page 123. Choose from the definitions below. Write the letter on the line.*

___c___   1. I was going to bake a cake this morning. However, I was <u>short on</u> eggs, so I made cookies instead.

_____   2. William has red hair, just like his brothers. Red hair <u>runs in his family</u>.

_____   3. I can't work on this project right now because I'm too busy. I'll have to <u>put it on hold</u>.

_____   4. Nancy got a raise in her salary. It was less than she'd hoped for, but it was certainly <u>nothing to sneeze at</u>!

_____   5. I'm not surprised that Anne became a professional dancer. She's been dancing all her life, so it's <u>in her blood</u>.

_____   6. Sabine wasn't accepted at Harvard University because her grades didn't <u>measure up</u>.

_____   7. I need to clean the kitchen. <u>On the other hand</u>, it's such a beautiful day that maybe I should work in the garden instead.

_____   8. The children really <u>look forward to</u> their birthdays. They know they'll have cake and get presents.

a. from a different viewpoint

b. part of one's character

c. not having enough of something

d. to meet someone's expectations; to be good enough for something

e. to be a characteristic learned or inherited from one's family

f. to be excited about a future event

g. to postpone something

h. quite good; fairly impressive

PRACTICING THE IDIOMS

D. Choosing the Best Answer

Listen to the pairs of sentences. The first sentence uses one of the idioms from this chapter. If the sentences are similar in meaning, circle SIMILAR. If they are different, circle DIFFERENT.

1. (SIMILAR) / DIFFERENT   5. SIMILAR / DIFFERENT

2. SIMILAR / DIFFERENT   6. SIMILAR / DIFFERENT

3. SIMILAR / DIFFERENT   7. SIMILAR / DIFFERENT

4. SIMILAR / DIFFERENT   8. SIMILAR / DIFFERENT

E. Retelling the Story

Read the script of The Fortune-Teller *on page 123 again. The sentences below refer to statements in that script. Restate the sentences, using the appropriate idioms. Try to write them __without__ looking at the story again.*

1. I didn't have enough money to see the fortune-teller.

   I was short on cash, so I told the fortune-teller that I'd see her another time.

2. The fortune-teller said I could expect to become wealthy.

   _____

3. She said my current job was not good enough.

   _____

4. She said I had a natural talent for art.

   _____

5. I said other members of my family had also been artists.

   _____

6. She said I would have to postpone doing many things.

   _____

7. She said I would have a fairly significant opportunity.

   _____

8. I probably wasted my money. But, from another viewpoint, what if she's right?

   _____

F. Putting the Idioms into Practice

Lauren is discussing a job offer with her friend Matthew. Read their conversation. Complete the sentences with appropriate idioms from the list below.

in my blood	**on the other hand**
looking forward to	**put that on hold**
measure up	**runs in the family**
nothing to sneeze at	**short on**

MATTHEW: Congratulations, Lauren! I heard you got a job offer from MicroCompute. That's great!

LAUREN: Well, thanks, but I don't know if I should take it.

MATTHEW: Why not? Didn't they offer you a good enough salary?

LAUREN: Oh, sure. The money is _____nothing to sneeze at_____.
1.

MATTHEW: So what's the problem?

LAUREN: The problem is that I was planning to go back to college, and I would

have to _____ for a while. I was really
2.

_____ being a student for a while. I'm not sure
3.

I'm ready to go to work full time.

MATTHEW: It's true that having a college degree is important. Without it you might

not _____ if you have a chance for a job
4.

promotion later on.

LAUREN: Yes, but _____ , this is the career that I was going
5.

to study for. I've worked with computers since I was a child. They're

_____.
6.

MATTHEW: And MicroCompute is a great company to work for.

LAUREN: I know, I know—that's what my father says. He wants me to take this job,

too. He also works with computers. I guess it _____.
7.

MATTHEW: Hey, do you think you could go to school and work at the same time?

LAUREN: No way. I'm already _____ time. With a full-time
8.

job, going to school would be impossible.

MATTHEW: Well, good luck making your decision. I'm sure you'll do the right thing.

II Finding the Idioms in Ads

INTERPRETING THE ADS

Look at the following ads. Determine what is being advertised. Find the featured idiom in each ad and review its meaning. Then answer the questions.

1. Describe the picture. Where is the woman? What is she doing?

2. According to this ad, what should every passenger *look forward to?*

3. Is the phrase *look forward to* used literally, idiomatically, or both ways? Explain.

WE BELIEVE ALL PASSENGERS DESERVE SOMETHING TO LOOK FORWARD TO.

At Virgin Atlantic Airways, we feel your vacation should start the moment you board the plane. That's why on every flight to London, you'll not only experience our renowned British hospitality, you'll also be entertained by a personal video screen right at your seat. Complete with a wide selection of first run movies, music videos, news, sports and even video games. No other airline offers economy passengers anything like it. Perhaps that's because when it comes to comfort, we believe no passenger should take a back seat. For more information or reservations, call your travel agent or Virgin at 800-862-8621.

virgin atlantic *Virgin*

Virgin Atlantic Airways offers all non-smoking flights to London's Heathrow from JFK, Newark, Los Angeles and San Francisco. To Gatwick from Boston, Miami, Orlando and Milwaukee (via Boston on Midwest Express).

Reprinted with the permission of Virgin Atlantic Airways.

This Offer Is Nothing To Sneeze At.

Save **$1.00** ON FOUR BOXES.
KLEENEX® Facial Tissue 175ct. Asst. Colors

Reprinted with permission of Kimberly-Clark Corporation.

1. *Kleenex* is a brand name for tissues, soft papers used for blowing one's nose. How are Kleenex and sneezing related?

2. What offer is Kleenex making?

3. What is the message of this ad?

1. At Christmas, it is customary to exchange gifts. Parents often tell their children that they must be good in order to receive gifts. According to the ad, what makes a great gift?

2. Explain the slogan *Makes a great gift. On the other hand, you've been very, very good this year.*

Makes a great gift. On the other hand, you've been very, very good this year.

The Bose® Wave® radio is the perfect gift for your favorite music lover. But listen to it once, and you may not want to give it away. After all, the Wave radio can fill any home this holiday season with amazingly big, full stereo sound. And yet it's small enough to fit on an end table, on a kitchen counter—just about anywhere.

There really is nothing like the Wave radio. In fact, *Popular Science* called it "a sonic marvel." Besides its unmatched sound, it has a unique array of features—a convenient remote control, pre-set station buttons, and many more. You can even plug in a CD or cassette player and enjoy your favorite pre-recorded music.

For more information, call 1-800-681-BOSE, ext. R9648. Be sure to ask about our in-home trial and 100% satisfaction guarantee. For $349, the Bose Wave radio will make your favorite music lover—who just might be you—very, very happy.

For free shipping, order before December 31, 1998.

Call 1-800-681-BOSE, ext. R9648.
For information on all our products: www.bose.com/r9648

Please specify your color choice when ordering the Wave® radio: ☐ Imperial White ☐ Graphite Gray
Mr./Mrs./Ms.
Name   (Please Print)   Daytime Telephone   Evening Telephone
Address
City   State   Zip
Or mail to: Bose® Corporation, Dept. CDD-R9648, The Mountain, Framingham, MA 01701-9168.

BOSE®
Better sound through research.

Ask about our interest-free six-month payment plan.

© 1998 Bose Corporation. Covered by patent rights issued and/or pending. Installment payment plan and free overhead shipping offer not to be combined with any other offer. Installment payment plan available on credit card orders only. Price does not include applicable sales tax. Price and/or payment plan subject to change without notice.

Reprinted with the permission of Bose Corporation.

1. What product is being advertised?

2. According to the ad, Dove is delicious chocolate that you should eat slowly. How does that relate to the slogan *Put the World on Hold?*

3. The line *You can't hurry Dove* is adapted from the song title "You Can't Hurry Love." Have you ever heard this song? What is its message?

4. What is the message of this ad?

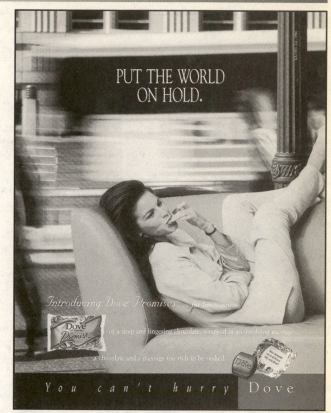

Printed with the permission of Mars, Incorporated.

The Quaker Oats Company.

1. What product is being advertised?

2. *Taste* means "flavor." It also means "good judgment about the quality of things." How do these two meanings relate to the slogan *Good taste runs in the family?*

3. In the last sentence, *It's the perfect addition to our family that your family will love,* who is *your family?* Who is *our family?*

This time of year, wine isn't just in my blood. It's in my hair and clothes.
GINA GALLO *Third-Generation Family Winemaker.*

In Sonoma, California's premier wine growing region, Gina makes international award-winning wines.

1998
WINERY *of* THE YEAR

San Francisco Int'l Wine Competition
2,800 wines entered from over 600 wineries

INTERNATIONAL
WINERY *of* THE YEAR

1998 Vinitaly Int'l Wine Competition (Verona)
1,482 wines entered from 22 countries

1998
BEST
CHARDONNAY
WORLDWIDE

Int'l Wine & Spirits Competition (London)
1995 Gallo of Sonoma Estate Chardonnay

GALLO *of* SONOMA
RUSSIAN RIVER VALLEY
Chardonnay

1997

1. *Gallo* is the name of a well-known brand of wine. Who is Gina Gallo?

2. Describe the picture. What is Gina doing?

3. Explain Gina's statement. How does it relate to the picture?

THINKING ABOUT THE ADS

Review the ads in this chapter. Choose the one that you like best. Complete the following statements based on that ad.

1. The ad that I like the best is . . . because . . . .

2. I think Americans would like this ad because . . . .

3. It is important to many Americans to . . . .

4. Other examples in American life that show how Americans feel about this value are . . . .

5. People from my country would/would not like this ad because . . . .

III Using the Idioms

USING THE IDIOMS IN SPEECH

A. Name That Idiom!

Play the following game in pairs. Try to be the first pair in your class to finish.

1. With a partner, copy the idioms from the list on page 120 onto separate index cards.

2. Divide the cards into two piles. Give one pile to your partner. Do not look at each other's cards.

3. Choose one card from your pile. Give a definition of the idiom or a sentence that illustrates its meaning <u>without</u> using the idiom.

4. After identifying the idiom correctly, your partner chooses a card from his or her pile and gives a definition or sentence.

5. Continue back and forth until you and your partner have correctly guessed all the idioms.

B. Round-Robin Story

Complete the following story in small groups.

1. One student adds to the story that begins below, using one of the idioms from this chapter.

2. The next student continues the story, using another idiom from this chapter.

3. Continue until all the idioms have been used and the story has ended.

    Mrs. Arnold was forty-eight years old. Her husband had died several years earlier, and her two children had grown up. She'd never done anything extraordinary; she'd always lived a quiet life and put adventure on hold. But one morning, she received a letter . . . .

C. Role Play

Perform a role play in pairs.

1. Imagine that you are one of the characters at the top of page 132. You may refer to the script of *The Fortune-Teller* on page 123 for background information.

2. Write a script for a role play. Use as many of the idioms from this chapter as you can.

3. Practice the role play.

4. Perform the role play for your classmates.

CUSTOMER: It is five years after you first met with the fortune-teller. You are now a rich, successful, famous artist. You are happy with your career. However, you're not sure if you should marry the person you've been dating. Ask the fortune-teller what to do.

FORTUNE-TELLER: Give the customer advice about love.

USING THE IDIOMS IN WRITING

D. Writing with Idioms

Do you know anyone who has to make a decision about the future? The people below have to make difficult choices.

Write a paragraph describing each person below.

- **Brent:** His family has owned a bakery for more than fifty years, but he wants to do something different with his life.

- **Lorraine:** She thinks her nose is too big, but she isn't sure if she should have surgery to make it smaller.

- **Pauline:** She is eighteen years old and can't decide whether to go to college or travel for a year.

Use at least two idioms from this chapter in each paragraph.

E. Advertising with Idioms

Create an ad for a product or service.

1. Choose a product or service that you would like to advertise.

2. Determine your audience—the people most likely to buy your product or service.

3. Write a slogan for your ad, using one or more of the idioms from this chapter.

4. Decide on what picture(s) you will use in your ad.

5. Write the rest of your ad.

6. Present your ad to the class. Do your classmantes understand your use of the idiom? Would they buy your product or service?

REVIEW III

Chapters 7–9

I. What Should I Say?

Write a response to each question or statement. Use the idioms in parentheses.

1. Jack just bought a large home in the hills and two new cars. Where did he get the money? (someone's ship has come in, upper crust)

2. I got a terrible grade in science. I'll never understand it! (catch on, smart cookie)

3. I just won the Best Student Award! (way to go, nothing to sneeze at)

4. When I graduate, my parents are going to give me $1,000. (look forward to something, window-shopping)

5. Should I go to college or get a job? I can't decide. (right up one's alley, on the other hand)

6. I was just going to buy one dress, but I came home with six. Should I take them back? (get carried away, out of the question)

7. Tom is always protesting something. He's just like his father, isn't he? (go against the grain, run in the family)

8. If I go to Europe, I won't have enough money to buy a car. What should I do? (short on something, put something on hold)

9. I'm thinking about hiring Katrina to make the food for my next party. Do you think she'll do a good job? (make no bones about it, measure up)

10. I heard you're going to sing at Julie's wedding. Is it true? (word of mouth, chicken)

II. Idiomatically Speaking . . .

Play the following game in small groups. You will need some blank index cards, game markers (such as coins), and a die.

1. As a group, write the idioms listed below on separate index cards. Put them beside the game board on page 135, face down.

2. Choose a marker (e.g., a coin or similar object) and put it in the **START** square.

3. Take turns doing the following.

   • Choose an idiom card.

   • Roll the die and move the marker the number of squares shown on the die.

   • Make a sentence about the topic in the square. Try to use the idiom on your card in the sentence. (**Note:** "UP TO YOU!" means you can choose the topic.)

   • If you use the idiom on the card correctly, you get another turn.

4. The student who reaches **FINISH** first is the winner.

IDIOMS		
catch on	look forward to something	right up one's alley
chicken	make no bones about something	run in the family
cut the mustard	measure up	short on something
earn one's stripes	nothing to sneeze at	smart cookie
get carried away	one's ship has come in	upper crust
get over something	on the other hand	way to go!
go against the grain	out of the question	window-shopping
in one's blood	put something on hold	word of mouth

1 **START**	2 your house	3 your family	4 **UP TO YOU!**	5 work
10 art	9 science	8 music	7 your friends ←	6 the news
11 clothes →	12 learning English	13 **UP TO YOU!**	14 sports	15 food
20 hobbies	19 **UP TO YOU!**	18 the weekend	17 the weather ←	16 the future
21 books →	22 travel	23 animals	24 games	25 **UP TO YOU!**
30 **FINISH**	29 TV	28 holidays	27 school ←	26 transportation

Chapter 10

SMALL TOWN, BIG CITY

Idioms

DOWN–TO-EARTH

FOR THE BIRDS

GET ONE'S KICKS

GO BANANAS

GROW ON SOMEONE

HAVE A BALL

LET SOMETHING OUT OF THE BAG

TICKLE ONE'S FANCY

Where can little builders really go bananas?

The DUPLO® Zoo Collection. A colorful combination of blocks, animals and playful pieces preschoolers go wild for. From cubs to crocodiles, these oversized DUPLO pieces make it safe and easy for your little ones to build creations all their own. And because DUPLO blocks work with smaller LEGO® bricks, the fun never ends.

Ages 2-5

duplo LEGO **Built for little hands and big imaginations.™**

Reprinted with permission of Lego Systems, Inc.

I Learning the Idioms

WARMING UP

Complete the following activities in pairs or small groups. Compare and discuss your answers with your classmates.

1. Discuss small towns and big cities. What are the advantages of living in a small town? The disadvantages? What are the advantages of living in a big city? The disadvantages? Which do you think is better? Why?

2. Complete the following sentences:

   • People from small towns are _____.

   • People from big cities are _____.

   Compare your answers.

3. Imagine that you are planning to build a small town. You only have enough money to build eight of the facilities below. Which eight would you build? Why? Discuss your reasons.

department store	grocery store	school
hospital	gas station	police station
fire station	factory	sports club
park	movie theater	bar
restaurant	apartment building	bank

GETTING TO KNOW THE IDIOMS

A. Listening for Understanding

Listen to Joe and Bette describe their hometowns. Think about the following questions. Then discuss your answers in pairs or small groups.

1. Where is Joe from? What kind of a place was it?

2. What did they do in Cactus Springs for fun?

3. Where did they go if they wanted more excitement? What did they do there?

4. Where is Bette from? What kind of a place was it?

5. Why did she decide to leave? Where did she want to go?

6. Where did Joe and Bette meet each other? Why did they decide to stay there?

Can you find the cities and states that Joe and Bette mentioned on the map? What do you know about them?

B. Identifying the Idioms

The idioms listed below are used throughout the descriptions you just heard. Read the script of the descriptions on page 139. Underline the idioms. Number them on the list below in the order they occur. Try to guess the meaning of each idiom by looking at how it is used.

____ **down-to-earth**   ____ **grow on someone**

____ **for the birds**   ____ **have a ball**

____ **get one's kicks**   ____ **let something out of the bag**

____ **go bananas**   ____ **tickle one's fancy**

Small Town, Big City

JOE: My name is Joe. I come from Cactus Springs, Nevada. Not many people know about the town; it's a tiny place in the middle of the desert. The town only has one stoplight, a gas station, two stores, three churches, and one restaurant. But that's where I grew up.

When I was a teenager, my friends and I would get our kicks by racing cars down State Street after midnight. There wasn't much else to do except watch the one fuzzy channel we could get on TV. When we wanted more excitement, we would save up our money and go to Las Vegas. Then we would really go bananas. There was so much to see and do! We had a ball just walking around, watching the tourists and the bright lights. Sometimes I gambled, but I had to keep it a secret, because my parents didn't want me to waste my money that way. Usually, someone would let the secret out of the bag, and my dad would get angry and say I could never go back. But I always did.

Mostly, though, I just stayed in Cactus Springs and got bored. All my friends said that living in a small town was for the birds, and they couldn't wait to leave and go someplace really exciting— like Chicago, Illinois. Most people never left, but I did. One day, I just packed my bags and started driving east. But I never got to Chicago. Halfway there, I met a woman named Bette.

BETTE: I'm Bette, and I was born in Chicago. Chicago was a very exciting city when I was growing up. It was so big and busy and loud. There were huge stores full of beautiful things to tickle anyone's fancy. There were movie stars and businessmen and people from all over the world. I loved it!

After a while, though, I got tired of the noise and traffic. I used to dream of going to a small town like Cactus Springs. I found that the people in small towns always seemed friendly and down-to-earth, and life there seemed much quieter and more peaceful. Finally, I packed my bags and started driving west. But I only got as far as Tulsa, Oklahoma. That's where I met Joe.

JOE: Well, Bette and I got married forty years ago. We talked a lot about going back to Chicago or to Cactus Springs, but we never did. We just stayed in Tulsa.

You know, if you live in a place long enough, it grows on you. We like Tulsa—it's not too small and not too big. Now we think it's the best place to be.

C. Getting the Meaning

Look at the underlined phrase in each of the following statements. Pay attention to how the idiom is used, and try to guess its meaning. You may also refer to the script of Small Town, Big City *on page 139. Choose from the definitions below. Write the letter on the line.*

___d___   1. Leonardo diCaprio is my sister's favorite actor. Whenever she sees him, she <u>goes bananas</u>.

_____   2. Everyone likes Mrs. Spires. She's so friendly and <u>down-to-earth</u>.

_____   3. The children went to Disneyland and <u>had a ball</u>.

_____   4. When I first met Margaret, I didn't like her. However, after spending time with her, she <u>grew on me</u>.

_____   5. I told Henry not to tell anyone about my promotion, but he <u>let it out of the bag</u>.

_____   6. Marie loves chocolate, so I think these chocolate chip cookies will <u>tickle her fancy</u>.

_____   7. Jeff <u>gets his kicks</u> by riding his motorcycle in the desert.

_____   8. I hate math. I think it's <u>for the birds</u>.

a. practical and simple

b. to reveal a secret

c. worthless; stupid

d. to become very excited

e. to do something for fun or excitement

f. to interest or please someone

g. to gradually become better liked by someone

h. to have a lot of fun

PRACTICING THE IDIOMS

D. Choosing the Best Answer

Listen to the radio interview. Then listen to statements from the interview. Read the sentences below. Choose the sentence that best matches the statement you heard. Circle a, b, or c.

1. a. People in Belleville were working with the birds.
    b. People in Belleville were working very hard.
    c. Looking for work in Belleville was very hard.

2. a. Mr. Harris was working for the big shoe factory.
    b. Mr. Harris's project was in a bag.
    c. Mr. Harris is going to talk about the secret project on the radio.

3. a. There will be a ball at the old factory.
    b. People will have fun where the factory once was.
    c. The entertainment center will have many balls.

4. a. The food at the new restaurants will be very fancy and expensive.
    b. The food will be the same at all the restaurants.
    c. There will be many different kinds of food at the restaurants.

5. a. The children will have a lot of fun at the playground.
    b. The children can eat bananas at the playground.
    c. The children will be very excited about the bananas.

6. a. The older children will have fun skateboarding or roller skating.
    b. The older children can kick their skateboards or roller skates.
    c. If the teenagers go skateboarding or roller skating, they will be kicked out.

7. a. Belleville will grow a lot larger.
    b. Many people will grow up in Belleville.
    c. In the end, most people will like the changes in Belleville.

8. a. The future residents of Belleville will be interested in the earth.
    b. The future residents of Belleville will be simple and pleasant.
    c. The future residents of Belleville will be different.

E. Retelling the Story

Read the script of Small Town, Big City *on page 139 again. The sentences below refer to sentences in that script. Restate the sentences, using the appropriate idioms. Try to write them* without *looking at the script again.*

1. In Cactus Springs we would have fun by racing our cars after midnight.

   We would get our kicks by racing cars down State Street after midnight.

2. We would really get excited in Las Vegas.

   _____

3. We really enjoyed ourselves watching the visitors and bright lights in Las Vegas.

   _____

4. I didn't want my parents to know I gambled, but someone always revealed my secret.

   _____

5. My friends thought living in Cactus Springs was not good.

   _____

6. The stores in Chicago had many beautiful things that anyone would like.

   _____

7. I wanted to go to a small town where the people are practical and simple.

   _____

8. If you stay in a place for a long time, you will like it more and more.

   _____

F. Putting the Idioms into Practice

It's Saturday night. Rachel and Hank are trying to decide what to do for fun. Read their conversation. Circle the idiom that best completes each sentence.

RACHEL: It's Saturday night. What do you want to do?

HANK: I don't know. Do you have any ideas?

RACHEL: Why don't we go bowling?

HANK: Bowling? Yuck! Bowling grows on me / is for the birds!
1.

RACHEL: OK. Do you want to see a movie? There's a new comedy playing

downtown. Some of my friends saw it last weekend, and they

went bananas / tickled my fancy. They said it's great!
  2.

HANK: I hate comedies! Maybe that's how you

let it out of the bag / get your kicks, but it's not for me.
  3.

RACHEL: All right. Well, there's a Bingo game at the community center tonight.

If you won't let the secret out of the bag / get your kicks, I'll tell you
  4.

what the grand prize is.

HANK: Forget it! Bingo is for old people. It might

tickle my parents' fancy / go bananas, but not mine.
  5.

RACHEL: Well, I like Bingo. Maybe if you play a few games, it will

let you out of the bag / grow on you.
  6.

HANK: I don't think so. Maybe we should just go out for dinner.

RACHEL: Great! Let's go to that French restaurant. They have wonderful food and

good service. And it's not very expensive.

HANK: No, I don't like French food, and I don't want to go somewhere fancy.

I'd prefer someplace more casual and for the birds / down-to-earth.
  7.

Don't you have any ideas?

RACHEL: Hank, I've got lots of ideas, but you don't like any of them. You can find

something to do by yourself. I'm going out tonight and I'm going

to grow on you / have a ball. But not with you! Good-bye.
  8.

II Finding the Idioms in Ads

INTERPRETING THE ADS

Look at the following ads. Determine what is being advertised. Find the featured idiom in each ad and review its meaning. Then answer the questions.

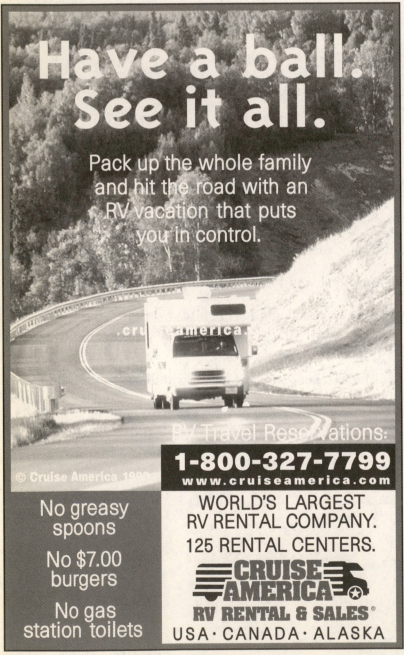

Have a ball. See it all.

Pack up the whole family and hit the road with an RV vacation that puts you in control.

.cruiseamerica.

RV Travel Reservations:

1-800-327-7799
www.cruiseamerica.com

No greasy spoons

No $7.00 burgers

No gas station toilets

WORLD'S LARGEST RV RENTAL COMPANY. 125 RENTAL CENTERS.

CRUISE AMERICA RV RENTAL & SALES®
USA · CANADA · ALASKA

© Cruise America 1999

Reprinted with the permission of Cruise America, Inc.

1. This ad is for a company that rents RVs, or "recreational vehicles." What is a recreational vehicle?

2. A *greasy spoon* is a "cheap, often dirty restaurant." According to this ad, what are the advantages of an RV vacation?

3. Explain the slogan *Have a ball. See it all.*

1. What is the name of the product? How does its name relate to its shape?

2. What idiom is used in this ad? How has it been changed?

3. The *Nutri* in *Nutri-Grain* is short for "nutrition." *To go* refers to food that is bought in a restaurant and taken away to be eaten. Explain the phrase *good food to go.*

KELLOGG'S ® NUTRI-GRAIN TWISTS is a trademark of Kellogg Company. All rights reserved. Used with permission.

Reprinted with permission of Lego Systems, Inc.

1. What product is being advertised? Who would use it?

2. Who are the *little builders*? How would they go bananas?

3. Describe the picture. How does the idiom relate to the picture?

The Best Way To Wrap Sandwiches Is Finally Out Of The Bag.

Reynolds Wrap™ is completely recyclable and costs less than plastic zipper bags, too.

Wrap it up right with Reynolds Wrap.

© R.M.C. 1993

Reprinted with permission of Reynolds Metals Company.

1. What has been used to wrap the sandwich in this ad?

2. According to the ad, what other product is used to wrap sandwiches? Why is Reynolds Wrap better?

3. Is the idiom in the ad used literally, idiomatically, or both ways? Explain.

Out-of-this-world resort

AT A DOWN-TO-EARTH PRICE.

Experience Palm Springs' most spectacular resort. Thirty-six holes of championship golf designed by Pete Dye and Gary Player. Tennis, health club, croquet, volleyball, Cactus Kids

FROM
$199
NOW THROUGH 4/17/93

Club and a water oasis with a 60-foot waterslide offer you a world of choices at a down-to-earth price. For reservations, call your travel consultant, 800-228-3000 or 800-999-8284.

 THE WESTIN MISSION HILLS RESORT
Rancho Mirage

Limited availability. Rates for room only, per night, double occupancy. Not applicable to groups, conventions, tours or other discount programs.

1. The idiom *out-of-this-world* means "extraordinary." How does this idiom relate to the idiom *down-to-earth*?

2. In this ad, what is *out-of-this-world*? What is *down-to-earth*?

3. What is the message of this ad?

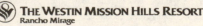

Reprinted with permission of the Westin Misssion Hills Resort.

1. This ad honors a teacher whose students learn math by studying birds. Explain the slogan *Mrs. Morse's students learn that math really is for the birds.*

2. Do you think this teacher really believes that math is *for the birds*? Explain.

3. The advertiser, an insurance company, presented the teacher with an award and gave her school $5,000. Why do you think the company did this?

Reprinted with the permission of State Farm Insurance Companies.

THINKING ABOUT THE ADS

Review the ads in this chapter. Choose the one that you like best. Complete the following statements based on that ad.

1. The ad that I like the best is . . . because . . . .

2. I think Americans would like this ad because . . . .

3. It is important to many Americans to . . . .

4. Other examples in American life that show how Americans feel about this value are . . . .

5. People from my country would/would not like this ad because . . . .

III Using the Idioms

USING THE IDIOMS IN SPEECH

A. Name That Idiom!

Play the following game in pairs. Try to be the first pair in your class to finish.

1. With a partner, copy the idioms from the list on page 136 onto separate index cards.

2. Divide the cards into two piles. Give one pile to your partner. Do not look at each other's cards.

3. Choose one card from your pile. Give a definition of the idiom or a sentence that illustrates its meaning <u>without</u> using the idiom.

4. After identifying the idiom correctly, your partner chooses a card from his or her pile and gives a definition or sentence.

5. Continue back and forth until you and your partner have correctly guessed all the idioms.

B. Round-Robin Story

Complete the following story in small groups.

1. One student adds to the story that begins below, using one of the idioms from this chapter.

2. The next student continues the story, using another idiom from this chapter.

3. Continue until all the idioms have been used and the story has ended.

Last summer I had the best vacation of my life. I had a ball! . . .

C. Role Play

Perform a role play in pairs.

1. Imagine that you are one of the characters below. You may refer to the script of *Small Town, Big City* on page 139 for background information.

2. Write a script for a role play. Use as many of the idioms from this chapter as you can.

3. Practice the role play.

4. Perform the role play for your classmates.

JOE/BETTE: Tell your seventeen-year-old grandchild about what you and your friends did for fun when you were his or her age.

GRANDCHILD: Tell your grandfather or grandmother about what you and your friends do for fun today.

USING THE IDIOMS IN WRITING

D. Writing with Idioms

Write an autobiography so that your grandchildren can read about your childhood.

Write two or three paragraphs about your childhood. Consider the following questions:

- What did you do for fun?
- What did you like?
- What did you dislike?
- Did you have any secrets? Did anyone find out about them?

Use at least four idioms from this chapter in your autobiography.

E. Advertising with Idioms

Create an ad for a product or service.

1. Choose a product or service that you would like to advertise.

2. Determine your audience—the people most likely to buy your product or service.

3. Write a slogan for your ad, using one or more of the idioms from this chapter.

4. Decide on what picture(s) you will use in your ad.

5. Write the rest of your ad.

6. Present your ad to the class. Do your classmates understand your use of the idiom? Would they buy your product or service?

Chapter **11**

FAME

Reprinted with permission of Tamron Industries, Inc.

I Learning the Idioms

WARMING UP

Complete the following activities in pairs or small groups. Compare answers and discuss with your classmates.

1. Write the name of a famous person for each of the categories in the chart. Then ask three other students for their answers. Write them in the chart, too. Compare your answers.

CATEGORY	Me	Student A	Student B	Student C
Actor				
Actress				
Athlete				
Author				
Historical figure				
Musician				
Political figure				
Scientist				

2. Would you like to be famous? Why or why not? If so, what would you like to be famous for? Why?

3. Imagine that you are TV writers and actors.

   - First, decide on:
     a. the type of show (e.g., action, comedy, love story, news program, soap opera)
     b. the location (e.g., island, street corner, train, hospital, house, restaurant)
     c. the characters (e.g., police officer, model, news reporter, rock star, criminal)
   - Assign the role of one character to each group member.
   - Write a script for *one scene* from the show.
   - Practice the role play.
   - Perform the role play for your classmates.

GETTING TO KNOW THE IDIOMS

A. Listening for Understanding

Listen to the audition for the role of Juliet in the play Romeo and Juliet. *Think about the following questions. Then discuss your answers in pairs or small groups.*

1. Why did the director seem angry and impatient?

2. What was wrong with Actress 1?

3. What was wrong with Actress 2?

4. What acting experience did Actress 3 have?

5. What happened when Actress 3 read her lines? How did the director react?

B. Identifying the Idioms

The idioms listed below are used throughout the audition you just heard. Read the script of the audition on page 153. Underline the idioms. Number them on the list below in the order they occur. Try to guess the meaning of each idiom by looking at how it is used.

____ cream of the crop   ____ judge a book by its cover

____ give someone a shot   ____ on the ball

____ go to great pains   ____ once in a blue moon

____ have something down cold   ____ one in a million

The Audition

DIRECTOR: Hurry up! What's taking so long? We've been here all day, and I still haven't found my Juliet! Where's the next actress? I hope she's good!

ACTRESS 1: Here I am, sir. What would you like me to do?

DIRECTOR: Do you know your lines?

ACTRESS 1: Yeah, I have them down cold: *(in bored-sounding voice)* "Romeo, Romeo, wherefore art thou Romeo . . . ."

DIRECTOR: She's terrible! They're all terrible! You haven't brought me one person who can act! Get me someone who's on the ball, someone who knows how to say these lines. Where's my assistant? Hey, isn't there anyone else?

ASSISTANT: Yes, sir. I've saved the best actress for last. She's very good, the cream of the crop. She's won many awards for her performances. I'm sure you won't be disappointed.

DIRECTOR: Fine! Then let me see her!

ACTRESS 2: *(in deep male voice)* Good afternoon. Shall I begin? "Romeo, Romeo, wherefore art thou Romeo . . . ."

DIRECTOR: Stop! Stop! I don't usually judge a book by its cover, but this "actress" has a moustache! What are you trying to do to me? Juliet with a moustache? Imagine what people would say! Get rid of him . . . or her. Whatever. Is that all? Isn't there anyone else?

ASSISTANT: Well, there is one more young lady here who insists on auditioning for the part. She's never acted before, but she's gone to great pains to learn her lines. Would you like to see her?

DIRECTOR: Oh, why not? I don't know what I'll do if I don't find an actress. We can't have a Romeo without a Juliet! I guess I should give her a shot. Tell her to come in.

ACTRESS 3: Hello, sir. Thank you for this opportunity. A chance like this only comes once in a blue moon. May I start?

DIRECTOR: Sure, go ahead.

ACTRESS 3: "Romeo, Romeo, wherefore art thou Romeo . . . ."

DIRECTOR: Perfect! Just perfect! She's one in a million! A wonderful actress! After this play, she'll be a star. She'll be in plays, in movies, on television, . . . and I don't have to worry about losing my job! Finally, I've found my Juliet!

C. Getting the Meaning

Look at the underlined phrase in each of the following statements. Pay attention to how the idiom is used, and try to guess its meaning. You may also look at the script of The Audition *on page 153. Choose from the definitions below. Write the letter on the line.*

___b___ 1. I met the president on my vacation. That only happens <u>once in a blue moon</u>.

_____ 2. Noelle's voice is like no one else's. It's <u>one in a million</u>!

_____ 3. I thought that man was homeless, but actually he lives in a mansion. I guess I shouldn't <u>judge a book by its cover</u>.

_____ 4. Elise runs three miles a day, hoping to get on your team. Why don't you <u>give her a shot</u>?

_____ 5. I'm very impressed with your assistant's skills. She's really <u>on the ball</u>!

_____ 6. I've been studying for the math test all week. I think I finally <u>have it down cold</u>.

_____ 7. Mrs. McMullin's students are <u>the cream of the crop</u>. Her class is the best in the school.

_____ 8. Harry's wife <u>went to great pains</u> to make a delicious meal for his boss. She was in the kitchen for hours.

a. unique; very unusual or special

b. very rarely

c. to form an opinion based on someone's or something's appearance

d. the very best

e. clever, capable, and efficient

f. to make a special effort to do something

g. to know or remember something exactly

h. to allow someone to try something

PRACTICING THE IDIOMS

D. Choosing the Best Answer

Listen to each performance at a piano competition and to the judge's comments that follow. Read the sentences below. Choose the sentence that best matches the judge's comments. Circle a or b.

1. a. This pianist gave it a shot.
    (b.) This pianist had the music down cold.

2. a. This pianist is one in a million.
    b. This pianist plays once in a blue moon.

3. a. This pianist practices once in a blue moon.
    b. This pianist went to great pains to practice the piano.

4. a. Mrs. Archer's students are the cream of the crop.
    b. Mrs. Archer's students perform once in a blue moon.

5. a. This pianist was really on the ball.
    b. The judge gave this pianist a shot.

6. a. The judge judged a book by its cover.
    b. This pianist went to great pains to dress for the competition.

7. a. This pianist is the cream of the crop.
    b. This pianist went to great pains to prepare for the competition.

8. a. This pianist had her music down cold.
    b. This pianist was on the ball to hide her mistake.

E. Retelling the Story

Read the script of The Audition *on page 153 again. The sentences below refer to statements in that script. Restate the sentences, using the appropriate idioms. Try to write them __without__ looking at the script again.*

1. Actress 1 had memorized her lines perfectly.

   Actress 1 had her lines down cold.
   _____

2. The director wanted a skilled and capable actress.

   _____

3. The director's assistant said that Actress 2 was the best.

   _____

4. The director didn't usually base his opinions of people on their appearance, but this actress had a moustache.

_____

5. Actress 3 had worked very hard to learn the lines.

_____

6. The director allowed Actress 3 to audition.

_____

7. Actress 3 said chances to audition happen very rarely.

_____

8. The director said that Actress 3 was unique.

_____

F. Putting the Idioms into Practice

Circle the idiom that best completes the sentence. Then finish the next sentence in your own words.

1. I'm sure Pamela will do well in her new job because she is very smart and capable. She proved that she <u>gave her a shot / spoke once in a blue moon / (was on the ball.)</u> When she <u>gave her presentation at the meeting, her supervisors thought it</u> <u>was great!</u>

2. I wasn't impressed with John at first because he isn't very good-looking. However, I knew that I <u>shouldn't judge a book by its cover / was the cream of the crop /</u> <u>was one in a million</u>. Now that I know him better, _____

_____

3. Tammy only travels by airplane <u>once in a million / once in a blue moon /</u> <u>when she has it down cold</u>. This is because _____

_____

4. We lost someone very special when Frank left last year. He <u>gave us a shot /</u> <u>judged a book by its cover / was one in a million</u>. Everyone will miss him because

_____

5. Please <u>be on the ball / give me a shot / go to great pains</u>! I promise I'll _____

_____

6. Jeremy had to memorize a poem for homework. He studied hard until he had it
<u>down cold / was the cream of the crop / gave it a shot</u>. When he stood up to
recite the poem, he _____

_____

7. Ben loves Maria a lot. He always <u>is the cream of the crop / goes to great pains /</u>
<u>gives it a shot</u> to please her. Yesterday he _____

_____

8. The service on PanGlobe Airlines <u>is the cream of the crop / has it down cold /</u>
<u>flies once in a blue moon</u>. It is the best because _____

_____

11 Finding the Idioms in Ads

INTERPRETING THE ADS

Look at the following ads. Determine what is being advertised. Find the featured idiom in each ad and review its meaning. Then answer the questions.

Some things happen once in a blue moon.

Other things occur even less often.

Accord Special Edition

How often does a car come along that includes a power moonroof, an AM/FM stereo with CD player, alloy wheels, power windows and door locks, cruise control, wood-grain-style trim, leather-wrapped steering wheel, security system with remote entry, automatic transmission and air conditioning, all at the equally uncommon price of $20,595? *Well, "rarely" does come to mind.*

MSRP excluding tax, license, registration and options. Dealer prices may vary. ©1996 American Honda Motor Co., Inc.   1-800-33-HONDA, ext. 946 and www.honda.com

Reprinted with permission of American Honda Motor Company, Inc.

1. According to the advertiser, is this an ordinary car? Why or why not?

2. Explain the slogan *Some things happen once in a blue moon. Other things occur even less often.*

3. What is the message of this ad?

1. What is usually found in the container in the picture? How does this relate to the idiom in the ad?

2. In this ad, the bank Downey Savings is advertising home loans. What else does the container look like?

3. What is the message of this ad?

THE CREAM OF THE CROP

When You're in the Market for a Bank!

Downey Savings and Loan Association, F. A.

Give a Girl a Shot!

Who knows, she may become the next Rebecca Lobo

By supporting the Women's Sports Foundation, you help provide girls and women with more opportunities to play sports. And playing sports gives them the chance to learn life lessons, like how to win, how to lose and how to be a team player. The kinds of lessons that count, whether the playing field is a basketball court or a corporate boardroom.

WOMEN'S *Sports* FOUNDATION

Eisenhower Park,
East Meadow, NY 11554
For more information call:

800-227-3988

Reprinted with the permission of Women's Sports Foundation.

1. This ad is for the Women's Sports Foundation, which helps give women chances to play sports. Rebecca Lobo is a professional basketball player. Explain how this relates to the slogan *Give a girl a shot!*

2. In basketball, a player *shoots a basket* or *takes a shot*. Explain how this relates to the slogan *Give a girl a shot!*

On the ROAD...

On the BALL...

On the GO.....

Think Wet Ones!

Clean up anytime...anywhere.

Reprinted with permission of Playtex Products, Inc.

1. Where is the girl in the first picture? What do you think *on the road* means?

2. What has the boy in the second picture been doing? Is the expression *on the ball* used literally, idiomatically, or both ways? Explain.

3. *On the go* means "very busy." Describe the third picture. How does the idiom relate to the picture?

4. Wet Ones are small, wet tissues used for cleaning. How could they be used in each picture?

1. What is being advertised? What is a *window pane*?

2. Explain the slogan *We go to great panes for your windows.*

3. Why did the advertiser spell it *pane* in the slogan?

We go to great panes for your windows.

Giving you our best. That's how we've become the largest vinyl window replacement specialist in Southern California. And an industry leader in door installations. You'll see it in our showroom, where you'll find the most comprehensive selection of Alcan, Great Lakes, Castlegate, IWP and other name brand windows and doors.

You'll feel it when you speak to our friendly and experienced home improvement consultants.

And you'll cherish it in the years to come. Because we're the only contractor who guarantees our expert installation for as long as you own your home. Every one of our products outclasses the competition in appearance, energy efficiency, noise reduction, security, and durability. Plus they're affordable for every homeowner's budget.

So visit our showroom today. With all our styles, colors and models of windows, patio doors, entry doors, garden and bay windows, you're sure to find exactly what you want.

And you'll meet people who really care about making your home improvement a rewarding and pleasant experience.

Dial ONE Window Replacement Specialists

Featuring **TRIUMPH!** World Class Vinyl Windows

1-800-266-6767
Visit our showroom, or call for a free no-obligation in-home estimate

Dial One WRS
Showroom Hours:
Mon-Fri 9-5
Sat-Sun 10-4

1529 E McFadden
Santa Ana

Fully insured Licensed/Bonded
No subcontractors Lic.#523043

FREE Entry Door
With the purchase of 5 installed windows (any type, any size ALCAN, Great Lakes or Triumph windows). Completely installed, including new jambs, casing, threshold, weatherstripping & lockset. Over 50 styles to choose from.

Offer expires 5-31-94 New customers only. May not be combined with other offers. Coupon must be presented at time of sale.

Reprinted with the permission of Dial One Window Replacement Specialists.

1. What is pictured in the ad? What product is being advertised?

2. *One's living* means "how one earns money," and a *shot* means a "photograph." Explain the slogan *If your living depends on that one in a million shot.* Who do you think the intended audience is?

3. The phrase *improve your odds* below the camera lens means "improve your chances." What is the message of the ad?

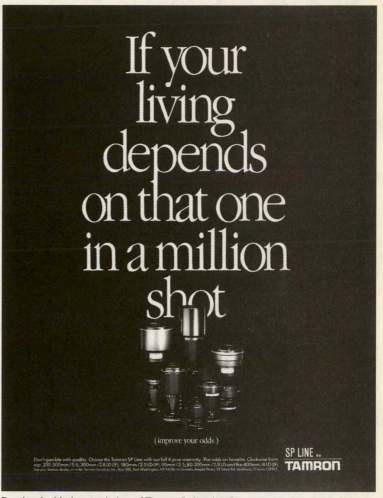

Reprinted with the permission of Tamron Industries, Inc.

THINKING ABOUT THE ADS

Review the ads in this chapter. Choose the one that you like best. Complete the following statements based on that ad.

1. The ad that I like the best is . . . because . . . .

2. I think Americans would like this ad because . . . .

3. It is important to many Americans to . . . .

4. Other examples in American life that show how Americans feel about this value are . . . .

5. People from my country would/would not like this ad because . . . .

III Using the Idioms

USING THE IDIOMS IN SPEECH

A. Name That Idiom!

Play the following game in pairs. Try to be the first pair in your class to finish.

1. With a partner, copy the idioms from the list on page 150 onto separate index cards.

2. Divide the cards into two piles. Give one pile to your partner. Do not look at each other's cards.

3. Choose one card from your pile. Give a definition of the idiom or a sentence that illustrates its meaning <u>without</u> using the idiom.

4. After identifying the idiom correctly, your partner chooses a card from his or her pile and gives a definition or sentence.

5. Continue back and forth until you and your partner have correctly guessed all the idioms.

B. Round-Robin Story

Complete the following story in small groups.

1. One student adds to the story that begins below, using one of the idioms from this chapter.

2. The next student continues the story, using another idiom from this chapter.

3. Continue until all the idioms have been used and the story has ended.

    David is a child genius. He started talking before he turned one, was reading by age two, and graduated from high school last year at the age of ten. Now he wants to go to the best university in the country, but the administration says he is too young to enroll. David's mother made an appointment to speak with the president of the university. She wanted him to give David a shot . . . .

C. Role Play

Perform a role play in pairs.

1. Imagine that you are one of the characters at the top of page 163. You may refer to the script of *The Audition* on page 150 for background information.

2. Write a script for a role play. Use as many of the idioms from this chapter as you can.

3. Practice the role play.

4. Perform the role play for your classmates.

ACTRESS: You are a famous, successful actress. You meet the director who gave you your first role as Juliet in the play *Romeo and Juliet* five years ago. You are grateful to him for giving you a chance. Ask him how he's doing.

DIRECTOR: It's been five years since you directed the play *Romeo and Juliet*. You used to be very successful, but now you are having a hard time finding work. You meet the actress who played Juliet in your play. She is now a rich, famous actress. Ask her for her help finding work.

USING THE IDIOMS IN WRITING

D. Writing with Idioms

Write a sales brochure for a newly invented product.

In a paragraph, describe an unusual new product. Possible products include:

• a mask that can change the shape of your face

• a spray that can make you invisible

• a medical test that can show exactly how much longer you will live

• a radio that allows you to "hear" what others are thinking

Explain why people should buy it. Use at least four idioms from this chapter in your paragraph.

E. Advertising with Idioms

Create an ad for a product or service.

1. Choose a product or service that you would like to advertise.

2. Determine your audience—the people most likely to buy your product or service.

3. Write a slogan for your ad, using one or more of the idioms from this chapter.

4. Decide on what picture(s) you will use in your ad.

5. Write the rest of your ad.

6. Present your ad to the class. Do your classmates understand your use of the idiom? Would they buy your product or service?

Chapter 12

LAW AND MARRIAGE

Idioms

BE AT THE END OF ONE'S ROPE

BREATHE EASIER

FACE-TO-FACE

HOLD SOMETHING OVER SOMEONE'S HEAD

PLAY SECOND FIDDLE

ROCK SOLID

RUN LIKE CLOCKWORK

TIGHTWAD

SO YOU NEVER

REACH THIS

←◉ POINT.

If you've ever reached the end of your rope with a car problem, you know why we designed Quality Care.

To make sure you get the best care possible, we spent 2 million hours last year training technicians on Ford, Mercury and Lincoln vehicles like yours.

We make sure all the necessary equipment is available to fix your car right the first time.

And when you have a question, your dealer has a Service Advisor with answers.

It seems to be paying off.

With higher levels of satisfaction from Ford, Mercury and Lincoln owners.

Quality Care at your Ford or Lincoln-Mercury dealer means you'll be back on the road. Not at the end of your rope.

FORD
MERCURY
LINCOLN

QUALITY CARE
Where the Quality Continues®

©1994 Ford Motor Company

Reprinted with the permission of Ford Motor Company.

I Learning the Idioms

WARMING UP

Complete the following activities in pairs or small groups. Compare answers and discuss with your classmates.

1. Some people who are getting married make a *prenuptial agreement*, a legal document with rules for when they are married and also if they get divorced. For example, if a rich woman marries a poor man, the prenuptial agreement might state that he won't get any of her money if they get divorced.

   Jane and Adam are getting married, but they are concerned about several issues in their relationship. They have decided to make a prenuptial agreement.

   • Read the issues below.

   • Put a check (√) next to those issues you think should be included in a prenuptial agreement. Put an X next to those you think should not be included.

      ____   Jane doesn't want to change her last name after they are married.

      ____   Jane has inherited a lot of money. She does not want to share it with Adam.

      ____   Adam owns his own business. He does not want Jane to own part of it.

      ____   Jane has a cat that she loves. Adam is allergic to cats.

      ____   Adam is very messy and never cleans the house; Jane is very neat and tidy, and does not like dirt or messes.

      ____   Jane has an excellent career. She does not want to stop working if they have children. Adam thinks that Jane should stay home after they have children.

      ____   Adam is a vegetarian. Jane likes to eat meat.

      ____   Jane wants separate bank accounts. Adam thinks they should have one joint account.

      ____   Adam thinks that he should not have to support Jane financially if they get divorced.

   • Compare and discuss your answers.

2. Do *you* think signing a prenuptial agreement is a good idea? Why or why not? Discuss your reasons. If a prenuptial agreement is made, what kinds of issues should it cover?

GETTING TO KNOW THE IDIOMS

A. Listening for Understanding

Listen to the lawyer explain how to decide whether to make a prenuptial agreement. Think about the following questions. Then discuss your answers in pairs or small groups.

1. What percentage of marriages end in divorce?

2. Why do some people think prenuptial agreements are a good idea?

3. Why do some people think prenuptial agreements are a bad idea?

4. According to the questionnaire, when should a couple make a prenuptial agreement?

5. How can the law firm help couples who want to get married?

6. How can the law firm help couples who are already married?

B. Identifying the Idioms

The idioms listed below are used throughout the lawyer's explanation you just heard. Read the script of the explanation on page 167. Underline the idioms. Number them on the list below in the order they occur. Try to guess the meaning of each idiom by looking at how it is used.

____ be at the end of one's rope   ____ play second fiddle

____ breathe easier   ____ rock solid

____ face-to-face   ____ run like clockwork

____ hold something over someone's head   ____ tightwad

Is a Prenuptial Agreement Right for You?

Welcome to the law firm of Nelson, Carter, and Barron. If you're thinking about getting married, consider this: Half of all marriages end in divorce. If you want to protect yourself from a difficult divorce in the future, our lawyers can help you write a prenuptial agreement.

A prenuptial agreement isn't for everybody. Some people think that it's a great idea and helps a marriage run like clockwork. Others say that it creates distrust in the relationship. To help you decide whether or not a prenuptial agreement is right for <u>you</u>, we've prepared a short questionnaire. Write the numbers one to six on a piece of paper. Then listen carefully to the following statements. Write either "agree" or "disagree" next to each one. Are you ready?

1. You think your relationship is very strong. You're sure that you'll have a rock solid marriage.
2. Your partner doesn't like to spend money. You think that he or she is a tightwad, and you want to be sure that the money in your marriage is distributed equally.
3. You think that the relationship between two partners is private. Disagreements between a husband and wife should be settled face-to-face, not by a lawyer.
4. Your partner has many other interests. Sometimes you worry that you will play second fiddle to his or her job or hobbies.
5. You believe in forgiveness. You would never hold a past mistake over your partner's head.
6. You'd breathe easier if the rules of your marriage were clear before you got married.

Which statements did you agree with? If you agreed with more even-numbered statements (numbers two, four, and six) than odd-numbered statements (numbers one, three, and five), then a prenuptial agreement would probably be a good idea for you. Our lawyers can help you with that process.

But remember, whether you sign a prenuptial agreement or not, 50 percent of all marriages fail. If your marriage isn't working, and you are at the end of your rope, we can still help you. If you're not happy with your partner, we can make sure you get exactly what you want.

C. Getting the Meaning

Look at the underlined phrase in each of the following statements. Pay attention to how the idiom is used, and try to guess its meaning. You may also refer to the script of Is a Prenuptial Agreement Right for You? *on page 167. Choose from the definitions given below. Write the letter on the line.*

___f___   1. Jake and Lucy decided to meet <u>face-to-face</u> rather than talk on the phone.

_____   2. Dennis had more experience in the business, yet he always had to <u>play second fiddle</u> to Nick.

_____   3. I'd <u>breathe easier</u> if I didn't live in an earthquake zone.

_____   4. Janice forgot her husband's birthday once, and he still <u>holds it over her head</u>.

_____   5. Don't ask Evan to lend you any money. He's a <u>tightwad</u>.

_____   6. Don't worry about this company. It's <u>rock solid</u>.

_____   7. My neighbor plays his drums late at night and wakes me up. <u>I'm at the end of my rope</u>!

_____   8. Maurice's new invention is perfect. It <u>runs like clockwork</u>!

a. to feel less worried about something

b. to be in a less important position

c. totally secure and reliable

d. to work smoothly without problems

e. to be unable to further endure a difficult situation

f. in each other's presence; in person

g. to continually remind someone of a mistake or fault

h. someone who hates to spend money

PRACTICING THE IDIOMS

D. Choosing the Best Answer

Listen to each short conversation between Julie and Rick and to the questions that follow. Read the sentences below. Choose the sentence that best answers each question. Circle a or b.

Conversation A

1. a. Fred doesn't trust Rick.
   b. Fred's business might not be very secure.

2. a. Julie would be relieved.
   b. Julie wouldn't breathe very well.

Conversation B

3. a. They talked on the phone.
   b. They talked in person.

4. a. He's very generous.
   b. He's not very generous.

5. a. It makes money selling clocks.
   b. It has no problems.

Conversation C

6. a. He couldn't endure it any more.
   b. He couldn't take any more rope.

7. a. Fred put his college degree in Rick's office.
   b. Fred didn't let Rick forget that he didn't have a college degree.

8. a. He didn't like the music in the office.
   b. He didn't like feeling less important than his coworkers.

E. Retelling the Story

Read the script of Is a Prenuptial Agreement Right for You? *on page 167 again. The sentences below refer to statements in that script. Restate the sentences, using the appropriate idioms. Try to write them <u>without</u> looking at the script again.*

1. Some people think a prenuptial agreement helps a marriage work smoothly.

   Some people say that a prenuptial agreement will help the marriage
   run like clockwork.

2. You are confident your marriage will be very secure.

3. You think your partner doesn't like to spend money.

4. You think arguments between a husband and wife should be resolved in person, without a lawyer.

5. Sometimes you worry you'll be less important than other things in your partner's life.

6. You wouldn't continue to remind your partner of a past mistake.

7. You'd feel better if you had clear rules for your marriage.

8. If your marriage doesn't work and you can't endure it any longer, our lawyers can help you.

F.   Putting the Idioms into Practice

Read the biography about Thomas Alva Edison. Complete the sentences with appropriate idioms from the list below.

be at the end of their ropes	play second fiddle
breathe easier	ran like clockwork
face-to-face	rock solid
hold it over his head	tightwad

Thomas Alva Edison's reputation as one of the greatest inventors in history is

_____rock solid_____. There will probably never be another person who
     1.

contributes as many inventions to modern living. His inventions include the light bulb,

phonograph, storage battery, cement mixer, and motion-picture camera.

Edison often worked for days without stopping, saying that he would

_____ when he could make his devices work. As a result, his
     2.

inventions almost always _____ . He even improved other
        3.

people's inventions. After Alexander Graham Bell invented the telephone, Edison

found a way to improve its ability to transmit sound.

Edison was much more interested in his work than in making money. Once he was

about to charge $3,000 for one of his devices. However, before he could ask, he was

offered $40,000! Edison was not a _____, and he spent most
        4.

of his money on more experiments.

Edison said that he could never understand mathematics or women. However, he did

get married twice and had six children. His family often complained that he spent most of

his time in the laboratory and that they always had to _____ to
        5.

his work.

When Edison was a boy, one of his chemical experiments caused a fire in a train. The angry train conductor hit him in the head and damaged his ears. Although he lost much of his hearing, Edison was not the kind of person to

_____. By the end of his life, Thomas Edison was nearly deaf.
                                 6.
Even when others spoke to him _____ in a loud voice, he
                                          7.
could barely hear them. However, he said deafness was not a problem, since the quiet

helped him concentrate.

Thomas Alva Edison patented more than 1,000 inventions during his lifetime. He succeeded with some of them after many, many failures. However, he was never discouraged. At a time when most people would be _____,
                                                                    8.
he said, "I have not failed! I've just found 10,000 ways that won't work."

II **Finding the Idioms in Ads**

INTERPRETING THE ADS

Look at the following ads. Determine what is being advertised. Find the featured idiom in each ad and review its meaning. Then answer the questions.

1. Chevron produces and sells oil and gas. However, this is not an ad for oil or gas. What is being advertised?

2. How does cleaning up the air help people *breathe a little easier*?

3. Is the slogan *Breathing a little easier* used literally, idiomatically, or both ways?

Reprinted with the permission of Chevron Corporation.

GEICO Auto Insurance.

Preferred by 9 out of 10 tightwads.

Buy direct from GEICO over the phone and you could save 15% or more on car insurance. 1-800-555-9129.

Reprinted with the permission of Geico Auto Insurance.

1. What is the advantage of buying GEICO Auto Insurance?

2. Why do you think the company advertises that *tightwads* like it?

1. Describe the picture. What *point* is being referred to?

2. Do you think this picture is effective? Why or why not?

3. What is the message of this ad?

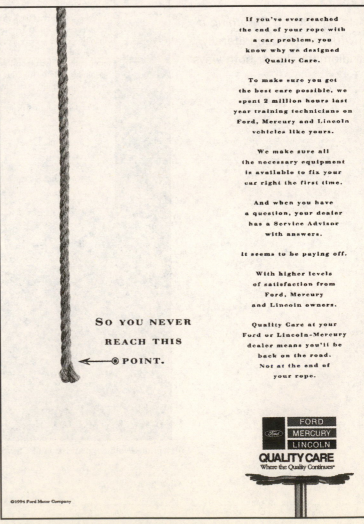

If you've ever reached the end of your rope with a car problem, you know why we designed Quality Care.

To make sure you got the best care possible, we spent 2 million hours last year training technicians on Ford, Mercury and Lincoln vehicles like yours.

We make sure all the necessary equipment is available to fix your car right the first time.

And when you have a question, your dealer has a Service Advisor with answers.

It seems to be paying off.

With higher levels of satisfaction from Ford, Mercury and Lincoln owners.

Quality Care at your Ford or Lincoln-Mercury dealer means you'll be back on the road. Not at the end of your rope.

SO YOU NEVER REACH THIS ← ⊙ POINT.

©1994 Ford Motor Company

FORD
MERCURY
LINCOLN
QUALITY CARE
Where the Quality Continues®

Reprinted with the permission of Ford Motor Company.

1. Describe the picture. What is the boy doing?

2. Explain the question at the top of this ad. What is Tech Corps worried about?

3. Tech Corps is encouraging companies to help students learn technology and leadership skills. How will that prevent America from *playing second fiddle*?

Reprinted with the permission of Tech Corps.

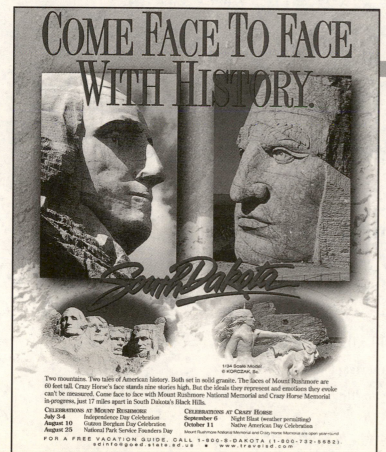

Reprinted with permission from South Dakota Tourism, Mount Rushmore National Memorial, and Crazy Horse Memorial.

1. Describe the pictures. What do they show? Where are they located?

2. What is being advertised?

3. Explain the slogan *Come face to face with history.*

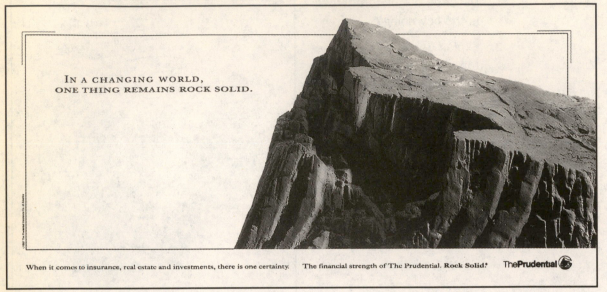

IN A CHANGING WORLD,
ONE THING REMAINS ROCK SOLID.

When it comes to insurance, real estate and investments, there is one certainty.   The financial strength of The Prudential. Rock Solid.®   ThePrudential

Prudential Insurance Company of America

1. Describe the picture. How does it relate to the slogan *In a changing world, one thing remains solid*?

2. According to the advertisers, what remains *rock solid*?

3. What is the message of this ad?

THINKING ABOUT THE ADS

Review the ads in this chapter. Choose the one that you like best. Complete the statements based on that ad.

1. The ad that I like the best is . . . because . . . .

2. I think Americans would like this ad because . . . .

3. It is important to many Americans to . . . .

4. Other examples in American life that show how Americans feel about this value are . . . .

5. People from my country would/would not like this ad because . . . .

III Using the Idioms

USING THE IDIOMS IN SPEECH

A. Name That Idiom!

Play the following game in pairs. Try to be the first pair in your class to finish.

1. With a partner, copy the idioms from the list on page 164 onto separate index cards.

2. Divide the cards into two piles. Give one pile to your partner. Do not look at each other's cards.

3. Choose one card from your pile. Give a definition of the idiom or a sentence that illustrates its meaning <u>without</u> using the idiom.

4. After identifying the idiom correctly, your partner chooses a card from his or her pile and gives a definition or sentence.

5. Continue back and forth until you and your partner have correctly guessed all of the idioms.

B. Round-Robin Story

Complete the following story in small groups.

1. One student adds to the story that begins below, using one of the idioms from this chapter.

2. The next student continues the story, using another idiom from this chapter.

3. Continue until all the idioms have been used and the story has ended.

    Mark was a poor but kind student. His girlfriend's father was a rich, successful businessman. Mark wanted to ask his girlfriend to marry him, but he was afraid her father wouldn't like him. Mark decided to meet her father face-to-face . . . .

C. Role Play

Perform a role play in pairs.

1. Imagine that you are one of the characters at the top of page 178. You may refer to Warming Up on page 165 and the script of *Is a Prenuptial Agreement Right for You?* on page 167 for background information.

2. Write a script for a role play. Use as many of the idioms from this chapter as you can.

3. Practice the role play.

4. Perform the role play for your classmates.

ADAM/ JANE: You love your fiancé(e), but you are worried about a few things. You want to make a prenuptial agreement before you get married.

LAWYER: Help Adam or Jane make a prenuptial agreement. Ask how he or she feels about some important issues.

USING THE IDIOMS IN WRITING

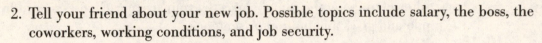

D. Writing with Idioms

Imagine that you got a new job.

1. Write an e-mail message to a friend.

2. Tell your friend about your new job. Possible topics include salary, the boss, the coworkers, working conditions, and job security.

3. Use at least four idioms from this chapter in your e-mail message.

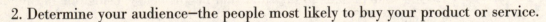

E. Advertising with Idioms

Create an ad for a product or service.

1. Choose a product or service that you would like to advertise.

2. Determine your audience—the people most likely to buy your product or service.

3. Write a slogan for your ad, using one or more of the idioms from this chapter.

4. Decide on what picture(s) you will use in your ad.

5. Write the rest of your ad.

6. Present your ad to the class. Do your classmates understand your use of the idiom? Would they buy your product or service?

REVIEW IV

Chapters 10–12

I. In Your Own Words

Read each paragraph. Rewrite the paragraph in your own words. Use at least three of the idioms suggested.

1. Ms. Overton was in charge of organizing a convention for 200 people. She worked very hard to make all the arrangements. Although it was difficult, she did an excellent job. The convention ran very smoothly, and everyone had a wonderful time. Ms. Overton was finally able to relax when it was over.

   IDIOMS: breathe easier, go to great pains, have a ball, on the ball, run like clockwork

2. Carlene's sister, Marlene, was prettier and more talented than she was. Marlene had won several awards, and she never let Carlene forget it. One day Carlene decided to enter a contest at her school. Although no one expected her to do very well, the judges allowed her to try. Carlene surprised everyone, including Marlene. She had prepared well and studied a lot, and she knew the answer to every question. She proved that she was one of the smartest students in the school.

   IDIOMS: cream of the crop, give someone a shot, have something down cold, hold something over someone's head, play second fiddle

3. Nancy's husband didn't like to spend money on anything. Although Nancy had fairly simple taste, occasionally she liked to buy something nice for herself. One day, she went shopping with her husband. She saw a very unusual and expensive coat, but she didn't think they had enough money to buy it. Later, her husband bought the coat. He kept it secret until Nancy's birthday, when he gave it to her as a present. Nancy was very surprised and happy.

   IDIOMS: down-to-earth, let something out of the bag, one in a million, tightwad, tickle one's fancy

II. Scrambled Idioms

Unscramble the idioms.

1. Read each phrase or sentence on page 180.

2. Think of an idiom that has a similar meaning to the phrase or sentence.

3. Unscramble the letters in parentheses to form an idiom with the same meaning as the phrase or sentence.

4. Write the idiom in the blanks.

1. very dependable (C K D S I O L R O)

 <u>r</u> <u>o</u> <u>c</u> <u>k</u> <u>s</u> <u>o</u> <u>l</u> <u>i</u> <u>d</u>

2. worthless and stupid (T R D S H E I B F O R)

 <u> </u> <u>o</u> <u> </u> <u> </u> <u> </u> <u> </u> <u> </u> <u>r</u> <u> </u> <u> </u>

3. work very smoothly (C R C K L I K L O U N W O R K E)

 <u> </u> <u> </u> <u> </u> <u> </u> <u> </u> <u>i</u> <u> </u>
 <u> </u> <u> </u> <u>o</u> <u> </u> <u> </u> <u> </u> <u>r</u> <u> </u>

4. stingy person (T H G T D I W A)

 <u> </u> <u>i</u> <u> </u> <u> </u> <u> </u> <u> </u> <u> </u> <u> </u>

5. really enjoy oneself (E L A H A Y A B L)

 <u> </u> <u>v</u> <u> </u> <u> </u> <u> </u> <u> </u> <u> </u> <u>l</u> <u> </u>

6. unable to endure something any longer (T R O E N E D N O F A S O T H E P E)

 <u> </u> <u> </u> <u> </u> <u>h</u> <u> </u> <u> </u> <u> </u> <u> </u> <u> </u> <u>o</u> <u> </u> <u> </u> ' <u> </u>
 <u> </u> <u>o</u> <u> </u> <u> </u>

7. Let him try. (A S O I G I Y E H I T M)

 <u> </u> <u> </u> <u> </u> <u>v</u> <u> </u> <u> </u> <u> </u> <u> </u> <u> </u> <u> </u> <u>h</u> <u> </u> <u> </u> .

8. I began to like it better. (T R E M E I O N G W)

 <u> </u> <u> </u> <u> </u> <u>r</u> <u> </u> <u> </u> <u> </u> <u> </u> <u>e</u> <u> </u> .

9. It really pleased me. (M I C K E I T Y C T F A N L Y D)

 <u> </u> <u> </u> <u> </u> <u>i</u> <u> </u> <u> </u> <u> </u> <u> </u> <u>e</u> <u> </u> <u> </u> <u> </u>
 <u> </u> <u>n</u> <u> </u> <u> </u> .

10. get very excited (B N A N O A A S G)

 <u> </u> <u> </u> <u> </u> <u>a</u> <u> </u> <u> </u> <u> </u> <u> </u>

11. very capable (H B L L T E A O N)

 <u> </u> <u> </u> <u> </u> <u> </u> <u>e</u> <u> </u> <u> </u> <u> </u> <u> </u>

12. know something perfectly (D W A O L T I C H N V E O D)

 <u> </u> <u> </u> <u> </u> <u>e</u> <u> </u> <u> </u> <u> </u> <u> </u> <u>o</u> <u> </u> <u> </u> <u> </u> <u> </u> <u> </u> <u>d</u>

Appendix A
GLOSSARY

A breeze (Ch. 1): very easy
Example: *The test was a breeze.*

A piece of cake (Ch. 2): very easy
Example: *This lesson is a piece of cake.*

Be at the end of one's rope (Ch. 12): to be unable to further endure a difficult situation
The possessive adjective must agree with the subject.
Example: *My son never listens to me; I'm at the end of my rope.*
A variation of this idiom is *get to the end of one's rope.*
Example: *Jennifer has too much work; she's getting to the end of her rope.*

Beg to differ (Ch. 5): to disagree
Example: *You might think that learning Russian is easy, but I beg to differ.*

Breathe easier (Ch. 12): to feel less worried about something
This idiom is often followed by *if, when,* or *after.*
Example: *We will all breathe easier after final exams.*

Catch on (Ch. 8): to learn; to understand
Example: *Using a computer isn't difficult. You'll catch on quickly.*

Chicken (Ch. 7): afraid or nervous
This idiom can function as an adjective or a noun.
Examples: *I'm too chicken to drive on the freeway. I won't drive on the freeway; I'm a chicken.*
Also note the idiom *chicken out,* meaning "to decide not to do something because of fear." Example: *I was waiting for the roller coaster, but at the last minute I chickened out.*

Come out of one's shell (Ch. 3): to become less shy and more sociable
The possessive adjective must agree with the subject.
Example: *Maisy was a shy child. However, when she got older, she came out of her shell.*

Couch potato (Ch. 1): someone who spends a lot of time sitting and watching TV
Example: *All Bart does is watch TV. He's a couch potato.*

Count on someone or something (Ch. 1): to depend on someone or something
Examples: *I'm counting on Eric to help me with my homework. I'm counting on his help.*

Cream of the crop (Ch. 11): the very best
Example: *The doctors at this hospital are the cream of the crop.*

Create a stir (Ch. 6): to cause a disturbance or excitement
Example: *The president's announcement that he was resigning created a stir throughout the country.*
A variation of this idiom is *cause a stir.*
Example: *The famous movie star caused a stir at the restaurant.*

Cut the mustard (Ch. 8): to be good enough
This idiom is usually used in the negative.
Example: *Jeremy was fired from his job because he couldn't cut the mustard.*

Do something for a living (Ch. 1): to do something as one's job
Example: *Mr. Collins writes travel guides for a living.*
A variation of this idiom is *make a living. Make a living* is always followed by a gerund.
Example: *Mr. Collins makes a living writing travel guides.*

Down-to-earth (Ch. 10): practical and simple
Example: *Although she is rich and famous, she is still down-to-earth.*
This idiom usually refers to people, but it can also refer to places, things, or ideas.
Example: *I don't want a large, expensive wedding; I prefer one that's more down-to-earth.*

Earn one's stripes (Ch. 8): to earn respect through hard work and success
The possessive adjective must agree with the subject.
Example: *I earned my stripes many years ago. Now I can relax.*

Eat one's words (Ch. 6): to admit that one said something wrong
This idiom is often preceded by *have to*. The possessive pronoun must agree with the subject pronoun; one cannot eat another person's words.
Example: *My friend said my speech was boring. However, after I won an award, he had to eat his words.*

Face-to-face (Ch. 12): in each other's presence; in person
Example: *I spoke with Luke face-to-face when he visited my town.*

For the birds (Ch. 10): worthless; stupid
Example: *Most of Jane's ideas are good, but this one is for the birds.*

Get carried away (Ch. 8): to lose one's self-control and do too much of something
Example: *I got so carried away with this project that I forgot about the meeting!*

Get one's kicks (Ch. 10): to do something for fun or excitement
Example: *My friends get their kicks snowboarding.*
A related idiom is *for kicks*, which means "for excitement."
Example: *They go snowboarding for kicks.*

Get over something (Ch. 7): to accept a difficult or surprising situation
When preceded by *can't*, this idiom often means "can hardly believe something."
Example: *I can't get over how much weight you've lost!*
This idiom can also mean "recover from." Note that you can *get over something* or *get over someone*.
Examples: *It was weeks before I got over my cold. It took me years to get over my last girlfriend.*
The related idiom *Get over it!* means "Accept it and move on!"
Example: *"This makes me so angry!" "Oh, get over it! It's not that important."*

Get something (Ch. 5): to understand something
This idiom is often used in the negative.
Example: *This assignment is too hard. I don't get it!*
It can also be used in a question.
Example: *Did you get his joke?*

Get the lead out (Ch. 4): to work harder or move faster
Example: *Get the lead out! We've got to leave now!*

Get to the bottom of something (Ch. 5): to discover the reason for something
Example: *I don't know why my computer isn't working, but I'll get to the bottom of it.*

Give someone a shot (Ch. 11): to allow someone to try something
Example: *Why don't you give Carl a shot? He might do a good job.*
Someone can be replaced with *something*. The idiom *give something a shot* means "to try something."
Example: *I've never tried Japanese food before, but I'd like to give it a shot.*
The related idiom *get a shot at something* means "to have a chance to do something."
Example: *If James wins the race, he might get a shot at the Olympics.*
Another related idiom, *give something one's best shot*, means "to try one's hardest."
Example: *I gave the competition my best shot.*

Go against the grain (Ch. 7): to behave differently than others
Example: *Ernie has his own way of doing things. He always goes against the grain.*

Go bananas (Ch. 10): to become very excited
Example: *Sam went bananas when he won the lottery.*
This idiom can also mean to behave in a crazy or out-of-control manner.
Example: *When I was out sick for two days, my boss went bananas and fired me.*

Go out of one's way (Ch. 3): to make a special effort
This idiom implies that one does something that one usually doesn't do.
The possessive adjective must agree with the subject.
Example: *When my car broke down, a man went out of his way to help me.*

Go to great pains (Ch. 11): to make a special effort
This idiom implies that one goes to a lot of extra trouble to do something.
Example: *I went to great pains to impress my boss.*
A variation of this idiom is *go to great lengths.*
Example: *I went to great lengths to find the missing book.*

Go with the flow (Ch. 4): to accept a situation without trying to change it
Example: *Don't worry about the audition. Just go with the flow, and you'll do fine.*

Grow on someone (Ch. 10): to gradually become better liked by someone
Example: *I didn't like this neighborhood at first, but it's grown on me.*

Hand it to someone (Ch. 5): to give someone credit for something
This idiom is often used with *have to* or *have got to.*
Example: *I've got to hand it to you. You did a great job!*

Hang out (Ch. 3): to spend time
This idiom can be followed by *someplace or with someone.*
Examples: *My son likes to hang out at the mall. He hangs out with his friends.*
Used by itself, this idiom can mean "to waste time not doing anything in particular."
Example: *"What are you doing?" "Oh, nothing. I'm just hanging out."*

Have a ball (Ch. 10): to have a lot of fun
Example: *We went to Disneyland and had a ball!*

Have a green thumb (Ch. 1): to have a special talent to make plants grow
Example: *Have you seen Helen's garden? She really has a green thumb.*

Have something down cold (Ch. 11): to know or remember something exactly
Example: *Manuel memorized the capital of each state. Now he has them down cold.*

Have time on one's hands (Ch. 4): to have extra, unscheduled time
The possessive adjective must agree with the subject.
Example: *When Mrs. Toomey has time on her hands, she knits.*

Hold something over someone's head (Ch. 12): to continually remind someone of a mistake or fault
This idiom implies an unwillingness to forgive or forget a past mistake.
Example: *After John cheated on a test, his teacher held it over his head for the rest of the term.*

In a jam (Ch. 6): in a difficult situation
Example: *I have two important meetings at 5:00. I'm in a jam.*
Contrast this idiom with *get out of a jam,* which means "to get out of difficulty."
Example: *I got out of the jam by rescheduling one meeting.*

In one's blood (Ch. 9): part of one's character
This idiom can mean that something is a unique part of someone's character.
Example: *Jane loves to act. Performing in front of an audience is in her blood.*
It can also mean that something is part of someone's character because of that person's family involvement.
Example: *Patrick grew up in a family of gardeners. Gardening is in his blood.*

Judge a book by its cover (Ch. 11): to form an opinion based on someone's or something's appearance
This idiom is almost always used in the negative.
Example: *That restaurant looks simple, but the food is delicious. I guess you can't judge a book by its cover.*

Kick the habit (Ch. 2): to quit an addictive behavior pattern
Example: *I've been smoking for ten years, and I can't kick the habit.*

Knock one's socks off (Ch. 3): to greatly impress one
Example: *Sean made a dish that knocked my socks off. It was delicious!*

Leave well enough alone (Ch. 1): to be satisfied with things as they are; to not try to improve things
This idiom is often used in the negative.
Example: *The soup was fine, but he couldn't leave well enough alone. He kept adding salt and spices until it was ruined.*
A variation of this idiom is *let well enough alone.*
Example: *Mrs. Cannon keeps rewriting the article. She can't let well enough alone.*

Let something out of the bag (Ch. 10): to reveal a secret
Something usually refers to a secret.
Example: *I'll tell you a secret, but don't let it out of the bag.*

A variation of this idiom is *let the cat out of the bag.*
Example: *It was supposed to be a surprise party, but someone let the cat out of the bag.*

Lighten up (Ch. 2): to relax; to not get upset
Example: *Don't be so serious. Lighten up!*

Look forward to something (Ch. 7): to be excited about a future event
Example: *I'm really looking forward to our vacation this summer.*

Make fun of someone or something (Ch. 6): to ridicule
Example: *The children made fun of Jan because her socks didn't match.*
A variation of this idiom is *poke fun at something.*
Example: *The cowboys poked fun at the man who didn't know how to get on a horse.*

Make no bones about it (Ch. 7): to have no doubt about something
Example: *I will be president. Make no bones about it!*
This idiom can also mean "to speak openly about something." In this case, *it* can be replaced with an idea or issue.
Example: *The candidate made no bones about <u>his support of gun control</u>.*

Make something from scratch (Ch. 1): to make something (especially food) with basic ingredients, rather than from a prepared mix
Example: *I'm usually busy, so I rarely make things from scratch.*

Measure up (Ch. 9): to meet someone's expectations; to be good enough for something
This idiom can be used without an object.
Example: *The new furniture looks nice, but the quality doesn't measure up.*
This idiom can also be used with *to* and an object.
Example: *This pie is OK, but it doesn't measure up <u>to the pies my mother made</u>.*

Not one's cup of tea (Ch. 3): not something one enjoys very much
Example: *I don't think I'll go to the concert tonight. Concerts aren't my cup of tea.*

Nothing to sneeze at (Ch. 9): very important or impressive
Example: *Bree bought a secondhand car. It's not a luxury car, but it's nothing to sneeze at.*

On a roll (Ch. 4): having repeated success
The subject of this idiom is usually a person or people.
Examples: *Josie has been telling one joke after another; she's on a roll. Our team has won ten games this season; we're on a roll.*

On Easy Street (Ch. 5): in a worry-free state (especially about money)
Example: *After Jim won the lottery, he was on Easy Street.*

On the ball (Ch. 11): clever, capable, and efficient
Example: *Mrs. Graham can get whatever you want. She's really on the ball.*

On the other hand (Ch. 9): from a different viewpoint
Example: *I'd like to go out with my friends tonight; on the other hand, I really should stay home and study.*
Sometimes people say, *On one hand . . . but on the other hand* for contrast.
Example: *On one hand, I'd love to take a vacation. On the other hand, I need to save the money to buy a new car.*

Once in a blue moon (Ch. 11): very rarely
Example: *An opportunity like this happens only once in a blue moon, so you should take it.*

One in a million (Ch. 11): unique; very unusual or special
Example: *This necklace is one in a million.*

One's ship has come in (Ch. 8): someone has become rich

Example: *I won the lottery! Finally, my ship has come in!*
This idiom is often preceded by *when*.
Example: *I'm going to travel around the world when my ship comes in.*

Out of step (Ch. 2): different from usual beliefs or behavior
This idiom is often followed by the phrase *with something* or *with someone*
Examples: *Jane is an independent thinker. For example, her clothes are often out of step with today's styles. As a result, she is often out of step with her friends.*

Out of the blue (Ch. 6): unexpectedly
Example: *This package arrived out of the blue.*

Out of the question (Ch. 8): impossible
Example: *I'd like to go to New York this weekend. However, I'm too busy, so it's out of the question.*

Pay the price (Ch. 5): to be punished; to suffer the consequences
Example: *Katherine had to pay the price for driving too fast. A police officer gave her a ticket for speeding.*
This idiom can be shortened to *pay (for something)*.
Example: *I know you've been lying to my friends about me. You're going to pay for doing that!*

Pick up the tab (Ch. 3): to pay for something
Example: *I'll pick up the tab for dinner.*

Play second fiddle (Ch. 12): to be in a less important position
One usually plays second fiddle *to someone* or *to something*.
Examples: *Jane feels like she always plays second fiddle to her older sister. I'm tired of Billy's schoolwork playing second fiddle to sports. (Billy thinks sports are more important than schoolwork.)*

Play with fire (Ch. 6): to do something dangerous or risky
Example: *I think motorcycle racing is playing with fire.*

Pull the wool over someone's eyes (Ch. 5): to trick or deceive someone
Example: *I never thought John was cheating. He certainly pulled the wool over my eyes.*

Put something on hold (Ch. 9): to postpone something
Example: *When my fiancée got sick, we had to put the wedding on hold.*
The related idiom *put someone on hold* means to make a person wait, usually while on the telephone.
Example: *Mr. Collins can't come to the phone right now; I'll have to put you on hold for a few minutes.*

Right up one's alley (Ch. 7): perfectly matched to one's interests
Example: *I love learning about the stars. Astronomy is right up my alley.*

Rock solid (Ch. 12): totally secure and reliable
Example: *Fred and Anna's marriage is rock solid.*

Run in the family (Ch. 9): to be a characteristic learned or inherited from one's family
Example: *Good cooks run in my family.*
Unlike *in one's blood*, this idiom always refers to something that is learned or inherited from one's family.
Examples: *All of the Williamsons are doctors or nurses; an interest in medicine runs in their family. All of the Smiths are tall; height runs in their family.*

Run late (Ch. 4): delayed; likely to arrive or finish after the scheduled time
Example: *I'm running late. I'd better hurry or I'll miss the train!*
An idiom with the opposite meaning is *be on time*, meaning "be punctual."
Example: *Usually I'm on time for work. However, this morning I overslept, so I'm running late.*

Run like clockwork (Ch. 12): to work smoothly without problems
Example: *Rudy's business runs like clockwork.*

Run-of-the-mill (Ch. 1): ordinary; average
This idiom is always used as an adjective.
Example: *I didn't think the movie was that great. I thought it was run-of-the-mill.*

See red (Ch. 2): to become very angry
Example: *My mother sees red when I don't clean up my room.*

See right through someone or something (Ch. 5): to know the truth in spite of outward appearances; to recognize falseness
Examples: *I told my boss I was sick, but she saw right through me. She saw right through my story.*

Short on something (Ch. 9): not having enough of something
Example: *Can you lend me some money? I'm short on cash right now.*

Smart cookie (Ch. 7): a very clever person
Example: *I'm impressed that you could answer the professor's question. You're a smart cookie!*

Stay on track (Ch. 4): to do something repeatedly and consistently
Example: *I've lost fifteen pounds! I've got to stay on track so I can lose even more.*

Take something lightly (Ch. 4): to be less serious than one should be about something
This idiom is usually used in the negative.
Example: *The general doesn't take the threat of war lightly.*

Take someone or something seriously (Ch. 6): to believe or accept something
This idiom is usually used in the negative. If the *something* in this idiom is one word or a pronoun, it must be placed between *take* and *seriously*.
Example: *I don't take <u>him</u> seriously.*
However, if the *something* is a phrase, it can also be placed after *seriously*.
Examples: *I don't take <u>his comments about politics</u> seriously. I don't take seriously <u>his comments about politics</u>.*
Contrast this idiom with *take something lightly.*

Throw caution to the wind (Ch. 6): to do something dangerous or risky
Example: *I only had ten dollars, but I threw caution to the wind and spent it gambling.*

Tickle one's fancy (Ch. 10): to interest or please someone
Example: *Those shoes tickled my fancy.*
Two idioms with similar meanings are *tickle someone* and *tickle someone pink.* Both idioms are usually used in the passive.
Example: *Carolyn <u>was tickled</u> (OR <u>was tickled pink</u>) when her boyfriend sent her flowers.*

Tightwad (Ch. 12): someone who hates to spend money
Example: *Nathan is a tightwad. He never spends any money.*

To each his own (Ch. 2): to allow everyone his or her own preferences
The possessive adjective is not changed to agree with the subject; if the subject is female, *<u>his</u>* is still used.
Example: *I like meat, but <u>my sister</u> is a vegetarian. To each <u>his</u> own.*

Turn down (Ch. 3): to refuse or reject something
When the object is a pronoun, it is always placed between *turn* and *down.*
Example: *John invited me to dinner, but I turned <u>him</u> down.*
When the object is a noun or noun phrase, it can be placed either between *turn* and *down* or after *turn down.*
Examples: *I turned <u>his offer</u> down. I turned down <u>his offer</u>.*

Up in arms (Ch. 2): very angry and ready to fight
Example: *Many people were up in arms when the school was closed down.*

Up to someone (Ch. 4): someone's decision or choice
Example: *I would like to go to the movie tonight, but it's up to you.*

Someone can be replaced with another object pronoun or a person's name.
Examples: *It's up to <u>him</u>. It's up to <u>George</u>.*
This idiom can also mean that the person named is responsible for doing something.
Example: *It's up to Luke to get his homework done.*

Upper crust (Ch. 8): the richest or highest class of society
Example: *The Kleins are very rich. They're from the upper crust.*

Way to go (Ch. 7): Congratulations
This idiom is always spoken directly to the person being congratulated.
Example: *"That was an excellent presentation. Way to go!"*

What makes someone tick (Ch. 3): what makes someone behave in a particular way
This idiom is usually preceded by the verbs *know* or *understand.*
Example: *I wish I <u>understood</u> what makes him tick.*

Window-shopping (Ch. 8): looking at items in stores without buying them
Example: *When I have no money, I like to go window-shopping.*

Word of mouth (Ch. 7): by one person speaking to another
Example: *I heard the news through word of mouth.*

Work oneself into a lather (Ch. 2): to become agitated or angry about something others consider unimportant
The reflexive pronoun in this idiom must match the subject.
Example: *Although the stain on her dress was so tiny no one could see it, <u>Sylvia</u> worked <u>herself</u> into a lather over it.*

Appendix B

AUDIOSCRIPT AND ANSWER KEY

CHAPTER 1   CAREER

AUDIOSCRIPT

D. Choosing the Best Answer

1. Brett takes his children to the park every day. He doesn't want them to become couch potatoes.
2. The Harrisons knew they could count on the firefighters to save their house from the fire.
3. Evelyn makes dancing seem like a breeze.
4. Kent won some money gambling in Las Vegas, but since he couldn't leave well enough alone, he later lost it all.
5. Al is looking for a gift for his girlfriend, but he doesn't want to get some run-of-the-mill flowers.
6. We all knew Ellen had a green thumb when she won a prize for her roses.
7. Stewart's lasagna was everyone's favorite dish. As usual, he made it from scratch.
8. After playing football for a living, Tony decided to open a restaurant.

ANSWER KEY

C. Getting the Meaning

2. d   3. c   4. g   5. a
6. e   7. h   8. f

D. Choosing the Best Answer

2. a   3. a   4. a   5. b
6. b   7. b   8. a

F. Putting the Idioms into Practice

Possible Answers:

2. I'm very active. I'm definitely not a couch potato.
3. I love to cook! I make everything from scratch.
4. No, I know when to leave well enough alone.

5. You can count on me! I'm very punctual and hardworking.
6. Sure. I think it will be a breeze.
7. I'd like to be a chef for a living. I love to work in the kitchen.
8. Yes. I have a green thumb, and I like to garden.

CHAPTER 2   DEBATE

AUDIOSCRIPT

D. Choosing the Best Answer

1. What happened when the teacher caught you cheating on your test?
2. Do you think a woman will ever be elected President of the United States?
3. My life will be ruined if I can't buy a new dress for the party!
4. I enjoy playing golf, but my friends think it's boring.
5. Simone is learning English very fast.
6. Did Marjorie get very upset when the doctor told her what was wrong?
7. Everyone in the office is dressed in a suit except Thomas. He's wearing shorts and a T-shirt.
8. Henry had smoked since he was fifteen, but last year he finally quit.

ANSWER KEY

C. Getting the Meaning

2. g   3. d   4. h   5. f
6. a   7. e   8. c

D. Choosing the Best Answer

2. a   3. b   4. a   5. a
6. a   7. b   8. a

F. Putting the Idioms into Practice

2. To each his own
3. lighten up
4. out of step
5. kick the habit
6. work themselves into a lather
7. piece of cake
8. up in arms

CHAPTER 3   LOVE
AUDIOSCRIPT
D. Choosing the Best Answer
Part A

A: Hello?

B: Hello, may I speak with Judy?

A: This is Judy.

B: This is Michael Moore. I met you at the party last night.

A: Oh, yes, I remember you well. You helped me carry all my packages to the car, and then you went back for my coat.

B: Well, I'm glad I could help. Anyway, it was nice to have an excuse to leave. I don't usually spend a lot of time at parties. I prefer to stay home and watch TV after work.

A: I know what you mean. I don't like going to parties much either.

Questions:

1. Why does Judy remember Michael?
2. What does Michael like to do in the evening?
3. How does Judy feel about going to parties?

Part B

B: Well, tell me what you like to do. You said your packages contained art supplies. What kind of artist are you? I'm interested in getting to know you better.

A: Actually, I'm surprised you called. You seemed so shy at the party. You sat by yourself most of the evening.

B: I know. I'm usually quiet in a big crowd, but if I'm with only one or two other people, I'm much more sociable.

A: I'm the same way. In fact, I don't accept most party invitations. I'm not very comfortable around that many people.

Questions:

1. What does Michael want to do?
2. How is Michael different when he's with only one or two people?
3. What does Judy usually do when she's invited to a party?

Part C

B: Judy, the real reason I'm calling is that I wanted to ask you to go to a dance performance with me on Saturday night. There is one dancer in particular who is very, very good. She will really impress you.

A: That would be great. I'd love to go.

B: Good! I'll pick you up at seven. And don't worry about the tickets—I'll pay for everything. See you then!

Questions:

1. What does Michael think of the dancer?
2. What will Michael do about the concert tickets?

ANSWER KEY
C. Getting the Meaning
2. h   3. b   4. e   5. g
6. d   7. a   8. f

D. Choosing the Best Answer
2. a   3. a   4. a   5. b
6. a   7. b   8. b

F. Putting the Idioms into Practice
2. are not my cup of tea
3. come out of your shell
4. pick up the tab
5. hang out
6. knock your socks off
7. turn me down
8. what makes you tick

REVIEW I   CHAPTERS 1–3
I. Which One Does Not Belong?
2. a   3. c   4. c   5. b

II. Describing People
Possible Answers:

1. Mrs. Jones has a lovely garden. She must have a green thumb. She says that gardening is a piece of cake.
2. Eddie is angry. He's stuck in traffic again. All this traffic is making him see red. He's really working himself into a lather.

3. Janet is usually shy, but tonight she is coming out of her shell. When she hangs out with people she likes, she has a lot of fun.

4. Megan works in an office for a living. Her boss really counts on her to help manage the office.

5. My nephew's style seems a little strange to me. I just don't know what makes him tick. Anyway, to each his own.

6. Paul has asked Rosie to go out with him several times, but she's always turned him down. She thinks he's not her cup of tea.

7. Chef Jeff always makes the food he serves from scratch. That's why customers return to his restaurant. His dishes really knock their socks off!

8. Everyone is up in arms over the mayor's decision to rename the city. They think he should leave well enough alone.

CHAPTER 4   RESOLUTIONS

AUDIOSCRIPT

D. Choosing the Best Answer

1. A: I have to clean this house before 4:00. I'll never finish!
   B: Oh, come on! If you get the lead out, you can do it.
   NARRATOR: The man thinks the woman can finish by 4:00 if she works faster.

2. A: Hey, would you like to get a cup of coffee?
   B: Maybe another time. I'm running late!
   NARRATOR: The woman can't get a cup of coffee right now.

3. A: I quit smoking two weeks ago, but I really feel like having a cigarette now.
   B: If you just stay on track a little longer, soon you won't feel like smoking.
   NARRATOR: The man thinks the woman should continue smoking until she doesn't want to smoke anymore.

4. A: I sold three cars this morning! Now I'm going to lunch.
   B: Why leave now? You're on a roll!
   NARRATOR: The man is going to eat a roll for lunch.

5. A: Now that you're not working, what are you going to do with all the time on your hands?
   B: Are you kidding? After doing my housework, there's no time left!
   NARRATOR: The woman spends a lot of time doing housework.

6. A: Should I get chocolate ice cream or vanilla?
   B: I prefer vanilla, but it's up to you.
   NARRATOR: The man told the woman to get vanilla ice cream.

7. A: My doctor told me I should exercise more. Maybe I'll start in a couple of months.
   B: I don't think you should take your doctor's advice so lightly. You need to take care of yourself now.
   NARRATOR: The woman seems worried about the man's exercise program.

8. A: I was invited to a party, but I don't know if I should go. I get nervous when I meet new people.
   B: Oh, just go with the flow, and you'll have a good time.
   NARRATOR: The man thinks the woman will enjoy the party if she acts differently than the other guests.

ANSWER KEY

C. Getting the Meaning

2. e   3. g   4. b   5. d
6. c   7. a   8. f

D. Choosing the Best Answer

2. T   3. F   4. F   5. T
6. F   7. T   8. F

F. Putting the Idioms into Practice

2. take it lightly
3. up to you
4. run late
5. get the lead out
6. have more time on my hands
7. go with the flow
8. stay on track

CHAPTER 5   CRIME
AUDIOSCRIPT

D. Choosing the Best Answer

1. I told the teacher that Michael was cheating on the test. Michael said that I would pay the price for telling her.
2. Before the surprise party, my boyfriend acted like he forgot my birthday. He really pulled the wool over my eyes.
3. When Mr. Harris noticed that money was missing from his drawer, he said he would get to the bottom of it.
4. If I win the lottery, I'll be on Easy Street.
5. Mrs. Stallings acts like she really cares about poor people, but I can see right through her.
6. My grandmother doesn't get why some people dye their hair blue.
7. Joe thinks that Burger Barn serves the best hamburgers. I beg to differ.
8. I have to hand it to you, Marian. I never thought you could beat Paul at chess.

ANSWER KEY
C. Getting the Meaning

2. f	3. c	4. d	5. a
6. e	7. h	8. g	

D. Choosing the Best Answer

2. F	3. F	4. T	5. T
6. F	7. F	8. T	

F. Putting the Idioms into Practice

2. a	3. b	4. a	5. b
6. a	7. a	8. b	

CHAPTER 6   STRANGE STORIES
AUDIOSCRIPT

D. Choosing the Best Answer

1. A: You know, sometimes kids are not very nice.
   B: I know what you mean. My daughter, Catherine, has to wear glasses, and some of her classmates call her names.

2. A: What happened to Ed? I heard he's in trouble.
   B: He sure is. He was selling expensive jewelry, but some of his customers found out it was fake.
3. A: This new product will keep your plants green, even if they don't get any water.
   B: That will be great in places that are hot and dry.
4. A: Paul, that test tomorrow is very important. Don't you think you should study for it?
   B: I don't care. I'm going to do something fun tonight!
5. A: I heard that Mrs. Graham came to see you. I'll bet that was a surprise.
   B: It was. I hadn't seen her in years, and I certainly wasn't expecting her visit.
6. A: Karen's father told her she'd never make any money as a writer.
   B: Really? Last year her new book sold a million copies.
7. A: Warren is amazed that you really quit your job. Is it true?
   B: Yes. I kept telling him I would, but he didn't believe me.
8. A: The police are busier on holidays because so many people celebrate in dangerous ways.
   B: You're right. For example, a lot of people drink and drive on New Year's Eve.

ANSWER KEY
C. Getting the Meaning

2. c	3. a	4. h	5. b
6. e	7. d	8. f	

D. Choosing the Best Answer

2. b	3. b	4. a	5. b
6. a	7. a	8. b	

F. Putting the Idioms into Practice

2. took her seriously
3. created a stir
4. eat their words
5. threw caution to the wind
6. playing with fire
7. out of the blue
8. get out of the jam

REVIEW II   CHAPTERS 4–6
I. Questions and Answers
Student A:

1. a   2. c   3. g   4. e   5. d

Student B:

1. d   2. g   3. c   4. f   5. a

II. Idiom Puzzler
Across:

1. price   3. time   5. bottom
6. wool   8. seriously 11. get
12. eat   13. roll   14. fun
16. differ   18. through   20. jam

Down:

2. caution   4. flow   5. blue
7. lightly   8. stir   9. up
10. lead   13. running   15. fire
17. Easy   18. track   19. hand

CHAPTER 7   ADVICE
AUDIOSCRIPT

D. Choosing the Best Aanswer
Conversation A

A: How did you find out that Claire got married?

B: Word of mouth. Everyone was talking about it. Her parents will never get over it!

A: Why not? Don't they like her new husband?

B: It's not that. They think she's too young. But you know Claire. She always goes against the grain.

Questions:

1. How did the news spread about Claire's wedding?

2. How do Claire's parents feel about her getting married?

3. Does Claire usually do what other people do?

Conversation B

A: Hey, Ron, way to go! Everyone loved your performance!

B: Thanks, Susie. I'm glad you liked it, but I'm just glad it's over. Right before it started, I was chicken, and I didn't think I could do it.

Questions:

1. Why did Susie talk to Ron?

2. How did Ron feel before the performance began?

Conversation C

A: No, Jim, I won't do it!

B: Oh, Julie, please? This project is right up your alley. You'd do a great job!

A: Make no bones about it, I can't work with Malcolm. He's impossible! The answer is no.

B: Julie, I know Malcolm is difficult to work with, but he's a smart cookie. I think he could help you with this project.

Questions:

1. Why does Jim think that Julie will do a good job?

2. How does Julie feel about working with Malcolm?

3. How can Malcolm help Julie?

ANSWER KEY
C. Getting the Meaning

2. c   3. a   4. g   5. h
6. b   7. e   8. d

D. Choosing the Best Answer
Conversation A: 2. b   3. a
Conversation B: 1. b   2. a
Conversation C: 1. b   2. a   3. a

F. Putting the Idioms into Practice
Possible Answers:

2. You're a smart cookie. I think you should apply!

3. Don't let jealousy ruin your friendship. Tell him, "Way to go!"

4. You stopped dating her over half a year ago. Get over it!

5. There's no need to be chicken. If you try something new, you might like it!

6. Make no bones about it, taking drugs is a bad idea. Tell your friends to stop!

7. In this situation, it's a good idea to go against the grain. You'll learn more and feel better if you don't cheat.

8. You can't believe everything you hear by word of mouth. The rumor probably isn't true. I suggest you ignore it.

CHAPTER 8   LAST WISHES
AUDIOSCRIPT
D. Choosing the Best Answer
1. A: Do you know how to play checkers?
   B: No, I've never played before.
   A: Why don't you watch the first game? You'll catch on quickly.
   NARRATOR: The woman thinks the man can learn to play checkers easily.
2. A: Do you think you'll ever be rich?
   B: Oh, I know my ship will come in someday.
   NARRATOR: The woman will travel by boat.
3. A: Did you buy a gift for your parents' anniversary?
   B: I went window-shopping, but I couldn't decide.
   NARRATOR: The woman isn't sure what windows her parents will like.
4. A: I have several important meetings next week.
   B: So I guess leaving town is out of the question.
   NARRATOR: The woman cannot leave town next week.
5. A: All the students listen to Mr. Jones. Why is that?
   B: He earned his stripes helping failing students get good grades.
   NARRATOR: The students respect Mr. Jones because he has a high salary.
6. A: I thought you were only going to ride your bicycle one mile!
   B: I know, but I got carried away and went the whole distance.
   NARRATOR: The woman rode her bicycle more than one mile.

7. A: I'm taking piano lessons, but I don't like to practice much more than once a week.
   B: If you want to play the piano well, you have to practice. Once a week won't cut the mustard!
   NARRATOR: If the man practices once a week, he will become a good piano player.
8. A: I'm applying to Bridgemont School. Do you think I'll be accepted?
   B: Bridgemont? I thought that was only for the upper crust!
   NARRATOR: The man is surprised because the woman is very rich.

ANSWER KEY
C. Getting the Meaning
2. g   3. c   4. h   5. a
6. b   7. d   8. f

D. Choosing the Best Answer
2. F   3. F   4. T   5. F
6. T   7. F   8. F

F. Putting the Idioms into Practice
2. cut the mustard
3. his ship has come in
4. earned his stripes
5. catch on
6. window-shopping
7. upper crust
8. carried away

CHAPTER 9   PREDICTIONS
AUDIOSCRIPT
D. Choosing the Best Answer
1. A: There was enough food at the party for everyone, but they were short on drinks.
   B: Everyone at the party had a lot to eat, but not enough to drink.
2. A: "Ms. Graves, would you please put Mr. Gibbs on hold while I speak with the person on line 3?"
   B: Ms. Graves should ask Mr. Gibbs to hang up the phone so the person on line 3 can speak.

3. A: It rained for a week in Texas. The rain created floods in some places, but on the other hand, the farms needed it.
   B: The rain in Texas caused both good things and bad things.
4. A: Diane is not looking forward to summer because she can't fit into her bathing suit.
   B: Diane is very excited about going swimming in the summer.
5. A: The Johnsons don't live in a large house, but their garden is nothing to sneeze at.
   B: The Johnson's home has a nice garden.
6. A: Wendy showed that acting was in her blood when she performed in her first movie.
   B: Wendy proved that she was a bad actress in her first movie.
7. A: Politics runs in the Pippin family.
   B: Several members of the Pippin family have had political careers.
8. A: Most of the contestants were well-qualified. Unfortunately, Susan didn't measure up.
   B: Susan was not as tall as the other contestants.

ANSWER KEY
C. Getting the Meaning
2. e   3. g   4. h   5. b
6. d   7. a   8. f

D. Choosing the Best Answer
2. DIFFERENT   6. DIFFERENT
3. SIMILAR   7. SIMILAR
4. DIFFERENT   8. DIFFERENT
5. SIMILAR

F. Putting the Idioms into Practice
2. put that on hold
3. looking forward to
4. measure up
5. on the other hand
6. in my blood
7. runs in the family
8. short on

REVIEW II   CHAPTERS 7–9
I. What Should I Say?
1. Jack's ship came in when he sold his company for millions of dollars. Now he can live like the upper crust!
2. You'll catch on quickly if you keep studying. You're a smart cookie, and I'm sure you'll get a better grade next time.
3. Way to go! That award is certainly nothing to sneeze at.
4. You must be looking forward to that! Let's go window-shopping to plan how to spend the money.
5. That's a difficult decision. I think college is right up your alley. On the other hand, college is so expensive that maybe you should work for a while first.
6. You really got carried away! Keeping all six dresses is out of the question. Why don't you choose the one you like best, and take the rest back?
7. Yes, Tom and his father both like to go against the grain. I guess it runs in the family.
8. If you travel to Europe now, you'll definitely be short on money. Then you won't be able to buy a car. Maybe you should put your trip on hold.
9. Make no bones about it, Katrina is an excellent cook. I'm sure she'll measure up.
10. You can't trust what you hear through word of mouth. I was too chicken to sing in front of such a large crowd.

CHAPTER 10
SMALL TOWN, BIG CITY
AUDIOSCRIPT
D. Choosing the Best Answer
A: I'd like to welcome Mr. Harris, President of the Belleville Chamber of Commerce. Good morning, Mr. Harris.
B: Good morning. Thank you for inviting me to speak on your program.

A: Mr. Harris, fifteen years ago, Belleville was a growing city. Then the city started to die. What happened?

B: Well, as you know, many people in Belleville worked at the big shoe factory. When the factory shut down, they had to move away. Trying to find work in Belleville was for the birds.

A: What are you doing to create new jobs?

B: We've been very successful in bringing new businesses back to Belleville. We've also been working on a secret project, and today I'm going to let the cat out of the bag. In place of the old shoe factory, we're building a new entertainment center. People can go there and have a ball. There will be theaters, stores, and a nightclub. There will also be several new restaurants, so you can order whatever kind of food tickles your fancy. And at the center of town there will be a huge park with a playground for the children. The kids will go bananas! Older children and teenagers can get their kicks skateboarding or roller skating.

A: That sounds great! Do you expect any problems with the project?

B: We've heard that some of the long-term residents of Belleville like things the way they are, but we believe that the new and improved Belleville will grow on them. Of course, the best thing about Belleville is that, even with all the changes we're making, our people won't change. They'll still be friendly and down-to-earth. We think Belleville will soon be the best place to live in the country!

Statements:

1. Well, as you know, many people in Belleville worked at the big shoe factory. When the factory shut down, they had to move away. Trying to find work in Belleville was for the birds.

2. We've been very successful in bringing new businesses back to Belleville. We've also been working on a secret project, and today I'm going to let the cat out of the bag.

3. In place of the old shoe factory, we're building a new entertainment center. People will go there and have a ball. There will be theaters, stores, and a nightclub.

4. There will also be several new restaurants, so you can order whatever kind of food tickles your fancy.

5. And at the center of town there will be a huge park with a playground for children. The kids will go bananas!

6. Older children and teenagers can get their kicks skateboarding or roller skating.

7. We've heard that some of the long-term residents of Belleville like things the way they are, but we believe that the new and improved Belleville will grow on them.

8. Of course, the best thing about Belleville is that, even with all the changes we're making, our people won't change. They'll still be friendly and down-to-earth.

ANSWER KEY
C. Getting the Meaning
2. a   3. h   4. g   5. b
6. f   7. e   8. c

D. Choosing the Best Answer
2. c   3. b   4. c   5. a
6. a   7. c   8. b

F. Putting the Idioms into Practice
2. went bananas
3. get your kicks
4. let the secret out of the bag
5. tickle my parents' fancy
6. grow on you
7. down-to-earth
8. have a ball

CHAPTER 11   FAME
AUDIOSCRIPT
D. Choosing the Best Answer
1. That young man has memorized his music perfectly!
2. This pianist's music is definitely unique!
3. I'm sure this contestant almost never practices the piano. Her performance was terrible!

4. This pianist is one of Mrs. Archer's students. Her students are always the best.

5. This pianist wasn't registered in the competition, but we decided to let him play anyway.

6. This contestant was dressed in old jeans and a T-shirt, so I didn't expect him to be a very serious musician. I'm surprised he did so well!

7. Finding the time to play the piano isn't easy for this contestant, but I know she practiced a lot.

8. This pianist forgot part of her music, but she hid that so well that no one even noticed.

ANSWER KEY

C. Getting the Meaning

2. a   3. c   4. h   5. e
6. g   7. d   8. f

D. Choosing the Best Answer

2. a   3. a   4. a   5. b
6. a   7. b   8. b

F. Putting the Idioms into Practice

2. shouldn't judge a book by its cover; *Possible Completion:* I think he's very intelligent and charming.

3. once in a blue moon; *Possible Completion:* she is very nervous about flying.

4. one in a million; *Possible Completion:* he was always kind, gentle, and helpful.

5. give me a shot; *Possible Completion:* do a great job for you.

6. had it down cold; *Possible Completion:* remembered every word.

7. goes to great pains; *Possible Completion:* gave her a wonderful birthday party.

8. is the cream of the crop; *Possible Completion:* the employees are courteous and helpful.

CHAPTER 12
LAW AND MARRIAGE
AUDIOSCRIPT
D. Choosing the Best Answer
Conversation A

A: Fred wants to talk to you about a job.

B: Really? That's great! I've been looking for a job that pays better.

A: Rick, be careful. Make sure his business is rock solid. I don't trust him.

B: Don't worry. I'll examine everything very carefully.

A: Good. And I'd breathe easier if you also talked to some other people about Fred's business.

Questions:

1. Why is Julie worried?

2. What would happen if Rick talked to other people about Fred's business?

Conversation B

A: So you finally met with Fred face-to-face yesterday. How did it go?

B: Not very well. He's a tightwad. I'm not going to make as much money as I thought.

A: What about his business? How secure is it?

B: Oh, it runs like clockwork. There's no problem there.

A: I don't trust Fred, but whatever you decide to do, I'll support you.

Questions:

1. How did Fred and Rick discuss the job?

2. How does Fred handle money?

3. Why is Fred's business secure?

Conversation C

A: What happened? I heard you quit your job!

B: I was at the end of my rope. I couldn't take it anymore!

A: Why? Was it because of your salary?

B: No, no. It was because I never graduated from college, and Fred held that over my head. He always made me feel like I was stupid. I got tired of playing second fiddle to everyone else. So I quit.

A: Well, congratulations. I never did like Fred, and I believe you'll get a much better job without him.

B: Thanks. I should have listened to you from the start.

Questions:
1. Why did Rick quit his job?
2. How did Fred make Rick feel stupid?
3. What did Rick dislike about the job?

ANSWER KEY

C. Getting the Meaning
2. b   3. a   4. g   5. h
6. c   7. e   8. d

D. Choosing the Best Answer
2. a   3. b   4. b   5. b
6. a   7. b   8. b

F. Putting the Idioms into Practice
2. breathe easier
3. ran like clockwork
4. tightwad
5. play second fiddle
6. held it over his head
7. face-to-face
8. be at the end of their ropes

REVIEW IV   CHAPTERS 10–12

I. In Your Own Words
Possible Answers:
1. Ms. Overton had to plan a large convention, and she had to make sure that everything ran like clockwork. She went to great pains to organize everything. Because she is really on the ball, the convention was great. Everyone had a ball, and finally when it was over, Ms. Overton could breathe easier.

2. Marlene always had to play second fiddle to her prettier and more talented sister, Carlene. Carlene had won several awards, and she always held it over Marlene's head. Then Marlene entered a school competition. The judges decided to give her a shot even though no one thought she would win. Marlene studied a lot and had all the answers down cold. When she won, she proved to the school that she was among the cream of the crop.

3. Nancy's husband was a tightwad. Although Nancy's taste was quite down-to-earth, sometimes she wanted to buy something that tickled her fancy. Once when she and her husband went shopping, she saw a dress that was one in a million. She loved it, but it was expensive and she didn't think she would be able to get it. However, her husband secretly bought it. On Nancy's birthday, he let the cat out of the bag and gave it to her. She was really happy.

II. Scrambled Idioms
2. for the birds
3. run like clockwork
4. tightwad
5. have a ball
6. at the end of one's rope
7. Give him a shot
8. It grew on me
9. It tickled my fancy
10. go bananas
11. on the ball
12. have it down cold